# TRACES OF TRUTH

**Ciaran Prior** spent 32 years in frontline policing and now works as a motivational speaker. A lifetime of dealing with death, trauma and tragedy has provided him with deep insights and a unique perspective on the fragility of this life we live, as well as a profound knowledge of how suddenly and violently it can end. This is his first book.

# TRACES OF TRUTH

## A CSI INVESTIGATES LIFE AND DEATH

## CIARAN PRIOR

GILL BOOKS

Gill Books
Hume Avenue
Park West
Dublin 12
www.gillbooks.ie

Gill Books is an imprint of M.H. Gill and Co.

9781804580646

Design origination by O'K Graphic Design, Dublin
Typeset by Typo•glyphix, Burton-on-Trent, DE14 3HE
Edited by Liza Costello
Proofread by Geraldine Begley
Printed and bound in Great Britain by Clays Ltd, Elcograf S.p.A.
This book is typeset in 12/18 pt Minion.

For permission to reproduce text, the author and publisher gratefully
acknowledge the *Longford Leader*.

*The paper used in this book comes from the wood pulp
of sustainably managed forests.*

A CIP catalogue record for this book is available from the British Library.

5 4 3 2 1

*This book is dedicated to the memory of
Detective Garda Colm Horkan
and inspired by the memory of my uncle
Ciaran Murray, who died aged 14 years,
and my childhood memories of
Detective Garda John Morley.*

Because I could not stop for Death –
He kindly stopped for me –
The Carriage held but just Ourselves –
And Immortality.

Emily Dickinson

# CONTENTS

PROLOGUE ix

CHAPTER 1    THE TROUBLES    1

CHAPTER 2    GONE BUT NOT FORGOTTEN    17

CHAPTER 3    DEATH OF INNOCENCE    41

CHAPTER 4    THE ULTIMATE SACRIFICE    59

CHAPTER 5    TRACES OF TRUTH: TRACE EVIDENCE    75

CHAPTER 6    SUSPICIOUS MINDS    89

CHAPTER 7    NATIONAL TREASURES    107

CHAPTER 8    THE COLD FACTS OF LIFE    123

CHAPTER 9    MYSTERIES OF THE UNEXPLAINED    143

CHAPTER 10    EVERY CONTACT LEAVES A TRACE    161

CHAPTER 11    DEAD MAN WALKING    181

CHAPTER 12    SIG SAUER SADNESS    203

CHAPTER 13    DEATH IS NEAR, NOT FAR    217

CHAPTER 14    NOT HOW THEY DIED, BUT HOW THEY LIVED    235

CHAPTER 15    BETWEEN FOUR WALLS    247

CHAPTER 16    ANATOMY OF AN INVESTIGATION    257

CHAPTER 17    WHO DIES?    279

ACKNOWLEDGEMENTS    305

# PROLOGUE

The boy jumped out of bed early, excitement gathering as he walked briskly down the hill from his home towards the shore, the line of newly erected telegraph poles standing sentry, emitting a faint smell of creosote as he passed them by. It was still mostly dark as he looked back up the incline towards his house.

Breaking into a run when the slipway came into view, he soon skidded to a halt, sending pebbles plopping into the barely moving current. He walked a little further along the bank, edging carefully towards the mooring spot where the sturdy wooden 16-footer, recently restored to its former glory, was tethered to a post in the rushes. The timber footwell creaked and rocked gently as he stepped in and balanced his weight. At the stern, he ran his fingers over the raised gold leaf lettering that spelled 'Seagull' on the outboard motor's shiny black tank, his other hand resting gently on the tiller, the only sound a faint rustling in the rushes as some fowl roused. This was the part he most loved, the final stage of the anticipation that had been building all week.

He looked towards the bridge and the wide expanse of water beyond, the still surface reflecting the faint glow of the early morning sky. Soon it would be time. He cherished these final moments almost as much as the trip itself. Hunting and fishing on the big lake was such a treat, a taste of the outdoor life he had come to adore.

The sound of footsteps crunching on the gravel slipway and the aroma of his cigarettes signalled his uncle Liam's arrival. A man of great kindness, with a particular fondness for his nephew, Liam's deep understanding of the wildlife and ecosystems in the area made him the ideal mentor. Together, they filled the boat with the picnic and tackle to make that day even more memorable. Then they were motoring out onto Lough Ree, the open water ahead beckoning, as behind the engine propeller disturbed its stillness into a wide V pattern, which disappeared before reaching the shore. The day passed amiably, the young lad soaking up his uncle's fishing and hunting wisdom. Each enjoyed the other's company and the pleasure of a tasty picnic they shared outdoors on one of the islands. Yet finally, like all good things, this day too had to end. As they approached their berth beside the old bridge at Lanesborough, it was time for landing. His uncle jumped ashore, and the young boy carefully passed the neatly stowed fishing rods, bait boxes and food hamper to him.

It was while lifting the last item that the calm silence was suddenly shattered, and a stench of gunpowder filled the air. The boy cried out in pain as his arm and chest took the force of the blast. The shotgun trigger had caught in a footwell hook as he lifted it, causing it to discharge. Assistance from the local doctor soon arrived and the only car in the village rushed him to hospital. His name was Ciaran Murray. He was 14 years old, my mother's big brother and my uncle. It was 24 February 1952 when he died from his injuries. I was later named Ciaran in his memory, and even though I was not yet born, my connection with death had already begun.

Later, when I found out about a second Uncle Ciaran (my father's brother) dying as a baby, a fear arose in my young formative mind as to whether the very name itself was somehow associated with death. Was I too destined for an early end? At national school our choir sang at funeral masses and the sight of so many tragic deaths made a mark on me. I clearly remember belting out 'Nearer My God to Thee' from the elevated church gallery as the grieving families left the church with the remains, the smell of incense wafting upwards, and superstitiously praying that none of them would make eye contact with me. I can recall frequently being unable to sleep in the aftermath of yet another local tragedy, with visions of death and coffins filling my mind.

The story of the tragic events of February 1952 left an imprint on me, as did the seemingly endless tragedies in our community. However, it was another kind treat bestowed by an adult that convinced me of my uncanny association with mortality.

In July 1980, Ireland was stunned at the shocking loss of John Morley. One of the greatest footballers in GAA history, John was a constant on the Mayo senior team for 14 years and a friend and garda colleague of my father. He was known for his easy-going personality, quick wit and innate desire to help people. As with my uncle Ciaran years before, I too had a much-anticipated special day as a 10-year-old in 1978 when I got to accompany John to the Roscommon v. Kerry U21 All-Ireland football final at the old Hyde Park, Roscommon. Garda protection was customary at all live RTÉ outdoor broadcasts, so as to minimise the risk of subversive forces hijacking the event and declaring themselves the Irish government. John's specific duty that day was to secure the commentary box where the great RTÉ sports commentator Micheál O'Hehir was broadcasting live.

Entering the grounds, I got to see at close quarters John's giant status as a sporting hero. Passing through the crowds, everybody seemed to know him, and I felt a warm glow in the presence of this strong man with a friendly word for everybody who crossed our path. Close to the pitch, John insisted on stopping at a stall vendor where he purchased crisps and a bar of chocolate for me.

As we reached the back of the old stand, I looked up at the commentary box of scaffolding bars and a ladder leading to a plywood-type structure with a large opening to the front. Not the steadiest looking structure, and well short of present health and safety standards, I wasn't too worried that day as I climbed that ladder. The structure seemed to slightly sway as I stepped into the gantry with John following closely by, his brown sports jacket billowing behind him to reveal a leather holster and the black handle of his firearm, a reminder of the reason for his presence.

Micheál O'Hehir was already there checking his equipment, his features familiar from seeing him on television, his Pioneer pin prominently displayed on his lapel. He greeted me warmly but accompanied it with a gentle warning to stay quiet once the commentary began. I sat fascinated at the large headphones and strange microphone with a hooded mouthpiece as the two men chatted before the match started. The thrill of the game, the bird's eye view, the roar of the crowd and, especially, the kindness of John remain vividly clear in my mind to this day.

Just over a year and a half later, on 7 July 1980, John Morley was shot dead while on duty. While I was enjoying the second week of the school summer holidays and hanging out with my friends, a blue Ford Cortina pulled up outside the Bank of Ireland on Main Street, Ballaghaderreen, County Roscommon. The occupants were armed, masked and filled with deadly intent. Walking to the football field of our Boys' National School some 34 miles away, we passed the home of Garda Brendan Gilmore, a past pupil of our school and star Longford footballer of the 1960s and 1970s. At that very moment Brendan was lying face down on a Ballaghaderreen road, the cold steel single barrel of a pump-action shotgun pressed against his head. He had just responded to a call of suspicious activity at the bank building. Two warning gunshots rang out as the communications radio was ripped from his patrol car dashboard while he and his colleague lay there fearing for their lives.

A loud screech of tyres and the stink of burning rubber filled the air as the getaway Ford Cortina lurched wildly down Main Street, speeding towards the garda station and then u-turning around. Two of its masked occupants hung out the windows, shotguns pointing skywards, and as stunned onlookers nervously retreated, the raiders' triumphant cheers were accompanied by two more shots discharged into the air. They had bagged £35,000 in cash. Their car was abandoned and set alight a short distance away, where it was swapped for a replacement white Ford Cortina with a black vinyl roof.

By this stage, reports of the robbery had been received at Castlerea Garda Station and the patrol car on duty had responded immediately. Garda Derek O'Kelly drove, accompanied by Sergeant Michael O'Malley and Detective Garda John Morley, who was carrying an Uzi submachine gun. They stopped to pick up Garda

Henry Byrne, who was walking back towards the garda station to finish his tour of duty. Derek O'Kelly skilfully manoeuvred the navy Ford Escort patrol car through Castlerea Main Street, a blur of blue flashing lights and screaming sirens startling shoppers and motivating traffic to give way.

As the raiders were pulling away from Ballaghaderreen in the replacement car, the gardaí were approaching Loughglynn village before deciding on a five-mile cross-country route to the robbery site via the townland of Aughaderry. Just before Shannon's Cross junction, the fleeing raiders' progress was momentarily blocked by a gravel truck. Continuing at high speed towards the crossroads, the gardaí and raiders fatefully met.

The white Cortina rammed into the lighter Ford Escort patrol car at speed, the impact shunting it sideways. The Castlerea gardaí had been wrongfooted by reports that the getaway car was a blue Ford Cortina. The raiders took advantage of the confusion by jumping out of their car and immediately opening fire. The quiet country silence was shattered, the thumping metallic sound of heavy calibre rounds piercing the patrol car's metal frame and the crash of shattered glass filling the air. Henry Byrne died instantly from a fatal shot to the head.

Trying to flee, the getaway driver floored the white Ford Cortina into reverse, mounting the ditch and jamming the passenger door around a tree. He abandoned the car as his comrades took to the fields. John Morley, who had also been shot, returned fire from the Uzi submachine gun. He gave chase, his strength and fitness propelling his pursuit despite his injury. In an act of honour and decency which had terrible consequences for himself, he called on the raiders to surrender as they fled, reluctant to shoot them in the back. One turned, however, and opened fire, hitting John a second time. He collapsed to the ground, never to rise again.

Meanwhile back in Lanesborough as I cycled home on my bicycle, I was surprised to see my father's car approaching at speed. Usually a very cautious driver, he pulled in quickly beside me, a plume of dust rising as he skidded to a halt. I immediately knew something was up. Letting down the window he told me that John Morley and his colleague Henry Byrne had just been shot dead in the aftermath of a bank robbery. I stood stunned and unable to move as he sped away to join the investigation, my 12-year-old mind struggling to process the information. How could John be dead? The next few days passed in a blur of national grief and mourning, the constant television, radio and newspaper coverage rendering it surreal to my mind. At the time, a single murder would be front page news for days, but this was unprecedented, and the country was in shock. The images of the patrol car, large bullet holes and shattered windscreen were splashed over every newspaper. I vividly recall accompanying my father to John's house in the days after the funeral, a grievous sadness filling the air as I played outside with his son Shane. Frances, newly widowed, was welcoming through her sorrow, kindness personified. Yet in my child's mind, death was yet again always just over my shoulder and inexplicably linked to me.

Time passed, and this fear faded as I passed through my teenage years. I joined An Garda Síochána myself in 1990. In the nine years I spent working in Dublin, I attended the scene of so many deaths, and thus witnessed the fragility of this life we lead, with firsthand knowledge of how suddenly and violently it can be taken away. Death remained my shadow, even as the childhood experiences became substituted by a resignation towards the reality of death, which had now become such a large part of my own professional reality. On 12 January 1999, I transferred to Castlerea Garda Station and, as I stood at the entrance, was joined by a colleague also moving down from Dublin, Garda Colm Horkan. Exchanging introductions next to the commemoration plaque honouring John Morley and Henry Byrne, who themselves had been stationed there, I was struck by the strength and warmth in Colm's handshake and his clean-cut appearance. Twenty-one years later he too would also be shot dead, just a few hundred yards from where we were standing, by a man I had arrested in 2006 following a siege-style situation in which he had threatened his family and a number of us gardaí with a samurai sword.

In 2007, I was appointed as a crime scene investigator with responsibility for collecting evidence for analysis at crime scenes. My work was based on a founding concept of forensic science, Locard's exchange principle: 'every contact leaves a trace.' Each perpetrator of a crime brought something to a crime scene and left with something from it, and both could be used as forensic evidence. Over the next 15 years of my work life, I dealt with serious crime and death on a large scale. Violent and unlawful situations where it was evident that the cause of death was murder, as well as sudden and unexplained end-of-life scenarios which required experienced judgement calls. Fatal shootings, murder, suicide, fatal fires, industrial fatalities, farm fatalities, sudden and unexplained deaths and fatal road traffic collisions were my lived reality, alongside serious traumatic incidents of robbery, rape, aggravated burglary and non-fatal stabbings.

This book recounts some of the more significant instances of grief, tragedy and sorrow I encountered throughout my crime scene investigation career. Along with some relevant snapshots from my earlier frontline policing, they offer an inside glimpse into how this strange world shaped my view of life and living and provide an insight into the hard-earned lessons I learned, both professionally and personally, along the way. I seek to show how these experiences ultimately led to a transformation in my understanding of the true nature of death.

# CHAPTER 1

# THE TROUBLES

My earliest childhood memory of the Troubles is of a visit in the mid-1970s to my father's border hometown of Swanlinbar, County Cavan. Accompanying my father and uncle to nearby Enniskillen, I sat transfixed in the back of the car as we first passed through a garda and customs border checkpoint and then a second more comprehensive roadblock at Mullen, just a few hundred yards down the road. Armed British soldiers stood in camouflage fatigues and berets alongside Royal Ulster Constabulary (RUC) officers in bottle-green uniforms and shiny boots. I could feel the tension in the air as my father and uncle answered questions through their respective windows against the backdrop of armoured jeeps and trigger-ready automatic weapons.

As we drove onwards, there was a strong sense of being in an entirely different place. My uncle pointed at an area of higher ground where he said a mortar attack had taken place and I innocently asked what a mortar was. My uncle described engineered metal tubes mounted on a flatbed lorry that fired explosive rocket-type projectiles at selected targets. Looking out at the rubble, bricks, wood and slate of a bombed building, I tried to make sense of it all, fascinated at seeing real destruction in real life rather than on the TV screen.

Not long afterwards, I vividly remember being taken to my grandfather's grave at Killaduff Cemetery just outside Swanlinbar and walking the steep incline behind my father to where he lay. I was stopped dead in my tracks by a headstone that both frightened and captivated me. At the base of it was a small protruding statue of an eerily lifelike face and the inscription, 'Volunteer Patrick McManus, died 15 July 1958.' My father explained, 'He was on active service with the IRA in the border campaign when his bomb exploded, and he was killed, with his colleagues surviving.' I had no clue what a border campaign was, or active service, and my father didn't seem inclined to elaborate. Yet his voice revealed a strange mix of respect for Volunteer McManus and regret for the sacrifice of his life and the loss his family had endured. 'A terrible thing,' he said, his voice trailing off. I had seen on television and in reality the damage a bomb could do, but now I understood it in a very different way. As we walked away from where Volunteer McManus lay, I thought of the strange, fixed carved stone face mounted on his headstone and tried to picture him alive.

On other occasions, my cousins Martin and Patrick took me down the road from my uncle's house at Swanlinbar to inspect the border-crossing bridge which had been blown up by the British Army and to climb the mound of debris left behind. This needless destruction had inflicted additional hardship on the decent, law-abiding people of the area by adding many miles to their now-diverted northbound journeys. 'It's an unapproved road,' my cousins explained. During the Troubles, the British Army regularly blew up minor border-crossing roads, thereafter deeming them 'unapproved' for usage. I nodded as if I knew what that was.

But all of this paled into insignificance for Swanlinbar on 8 December 1974, the feast of the Immaculate Conception. St Mary's Catholic Church sat impassively, as it had since its construction in

1828, dominating the square and providing a focal point for the small border town. Deep inside it was dark, save for a small light that illuminated the Christmas crib, the wise men and sheltering family looking out across the shadowy aisles. The underside of one of the sturdy bench seats, however, housed something that did not belong. An imperceptible ticking signalled the advance of a timer counting down towards daylight, to when it would no longer exist, its purpose served.

At 8:00 a.m., the shockwaves and force of a massive explosion ripped through the church, a deafening roar shattering the silence for miles around. The stained-glass windows blew outwards, fragments travelling as deadly projectiles for half a mile, embedding in trees, buildings and anything in their path. The roof bulged upwards; slates launched airborne before the stricken joists crumpled to the ground. The old double entrance doors disintegrated and the brass door handles became airborne projectiles that landed across the bridge in front of the post office. The force reverberated outwards, creating shockwaves as flying debris blew in the windows and front door of the closest house, my grandmother's.

All that remained were the church walls, the tower and, remarkably enough, the tabernacle standing proudly untouched by the chaos. There were no injuries, but the church had to be demolished, and the new St Mary's Church was rededicated on 15 August 1978 with a floor unusually sloping towards the altar and a new seating capacity for 600 people. It was believed that one of the main Loyalist paramilitary organisations, either the Ulster Volunteer Force (UVF), Ulster Defence Association or Red Hand Commando, was responsible for the attack.

Decades later, I was working as a crime scene investigator at a burglary in Ardagh, County Longford. At a time before it became policy to close rural garda stations, the picturesque village had a small one-man outpost, Garda John Coppinger its sole occupant.

'You must be a son of Packie's?' he enquired, as we launched into a conversation about John's years of service in Swanlinbar in the 1970s. 'I was standing in your grandmother's when the bomb went off and the force blew me across the floor,' he recalled. 'I was renting a room from her, digs as it was known back then, and remember well the force of the blast. Your grandmother was a calm woman who took it in her stride even though the bomb debris reached her front door and shattered her windows.'

When I was taken to my grandmother's home in the spring following the bombing, my cousins and I quickly set about exploring the devastated scene. We climbed and explored the ruins and poked without fear through blocks, plaster, timber and glass piled in the random mayhem, trying to find the shape of anything familiar in the twisted wreckage. Crossing the debris, the remains of what once was a confessional box lay splintered underneath the fallen roof joists. A piercing pain suddenly shot up through the sole of my left foot as I stepped onto a protruding nail from a wooden plank, perhaps well-deserved for trampling across the consecrated ground. I was in a dilemma. Owning up to it would earn either one of two reactions: 'Good enough for you, weren't you told to keep out of there?' or 'That's it, we're going home now,' and the fun would be over. I decided on a policy of non-disclosure and hobbled through the rest of the evening, a red blood patch now darkening the light-blue material of my runner. I had never heard of a tetanus shot and was lucky to avoid infection over the next few days as the wound healed. Or maybe it was the holy water my grandmother doused us with as we returned to her front door, sweaty and dusty, the bloody runner and limp going unnoticed.

The UVF returned to Swanlinbar, detonating a bomb outside a drapery premises, Irish House, and a smaller one in the national school opposite my uncle's home. Nobody was injured and this time the school site was dutifully explored, my cousins reporting how, just shortly before the blast, they had spent hours playing in the yard now strewn with glass and debris. And so the Troubles continued throughout my childhood, with reports of death and destruction on an almost daily basis.

Although my home was just 44 miles from the nearest border crossing, the events in Northern Ireland felt like a world away for most of my friends and neighbours. Those visits to Swanlinbar and Enniskillen, however, helped me better understand just how close we actually were to the reality of the conflict. I also came to realise that my father was performing dangerous border duty as a garda detective with colleagues at Blacklion, Dundalk, Buncrana and Pettigo. They were trying to prevent further atrocities by keeping the UVF out of the Republic and the IRA from launching attacks into Northern Ireland. Sadly, the gardaí frequently faced the 'border cold shoulder'; they were perceived by some as betrayers of the republican cause and as representatives of the accursed 'Free State'.

The threat of parcel bombs was also very present during my childhood. My auntie Kathleen, a kind woman, still hale and hearty and now well into her eighties, frequently made her generosity felt at our home with packages sent from London containing toys and gifts. On arrival, they would be seized by my father who would carefully open them across the back garden wall for protection in the event of an explosion. Thankfully it never happened, but such were the times that we lived in. So many lives had been lost in the Troubles and my father was making sure we would not be added to that tally.

In the long hot summer of 1976, Auntie Kathleen and her husband Frank came to visit us for a week. Walking with them to the crowded banks of the River Shannon, I spotted a plastic boat with a red base and yellow top complete with funnels, similar to the Titanic, for sale in Tony O'Flaherty's shop window, the astute businessman responding swiftly to the needs created by the heatwave. Kathleen kindly bought it for me and I couldn't wait to play with it in the children's outdoor swimming pool adjacent to the river. Initially I sat in the shallow section, sailing my ship along the sloping blue incline to the deeper end. Before long the entire pool was a writhing, splashing mass of youthful exuberance. I watched in awe as one of the older lads, Francis Toner, sat on the corner of the railing and then pushed off, soaring through the air, clearing the surrounding path and somehow finding a vacant space in the water in which to land. Within minutes this was the thing to do, there were youngsters' bodies flying everywhere, mid-air collisions, banged heads and a tempest of water, so I retreated with my boat to where Kathleen had prepared a picnic on the sloping riverbank.

Suddenly, there was a commotion and a lady I didn't recognise came running along shouting, 'Help, help, can anyone swim? There's a man drowning.' Without hesitation, Uncle Frank jumped up and ran to the riverbank with her as she pointed to where the

8

man had gone in. I can still see his tanned muscular complexion as he plunged into the dark depths and, as I stood with Kathleen watching the spot where he had entered, I dreaded that he would never resurface. Frank reappeared a good 30 yards from where he had dived in, took a few deep breaths and went under again. This continued for what seemed like an age until he finally emerged exhausted, his efforts in vain. A silence descended on the gathering, the pool emptied and even the older kids stood silently watching as Frank pulled himself ashore and shook his head in the negative. The man had drowned; his body was recovered days later. On that idyllic summer's day, the hushed tones of the gathered onlookers cast a strange spell. The descending silence, stillness and sense of shock was something I would experience many times in the decades to follow at scenes of violent death.

As Kathleen gathered our towels and picnic remains, I was painfully aware that the tragic death of my namesake, Uncle Ciaran, had happened on the opposite bank of the river from where Frank now dried off. Life's reality was encapsulated in that midday scene: stunning natural beauty, magnificent weather, unbridled youthful exuberance and joy, then suddenly calamitous death intervening, with its lull and hush still hanging heavy in the air. The sun remained high in a searing blue sky, unmoved by events below and, as I looked back down from the bridge, half dreading, half drawn to the view, I made out a bicycle lying on the slip, its owner never to return. There was to be no happy ending here as we continued across the bridge, still looking back and with my boat safely tucked under my arm.

◆

Eamon Masterson, a proud member of the Irish Defence Forces, died tragically in a road traffic accident on 20 March 1978. His son Eamon Junior was a friend and classmate in primary school and it was a lonesome and heartbreaking sight for us singing the funeral mass above in the church gallery as our friend walked behind his father's tricolour-draped remains. Then, before we knew it, on 4 June 1978, Eamon's next-door neighbour Ned Tynan, only 19, lost his life in another fatal car crash and we looked down once more on a devastated family as yet again we sang the requiem mass. This was life at its very cruellest; three years beforehand on 27 December 1975, Ned's brother Jimmy, had been killed after being struck by a car. These deaths seemed relentless.

Michael Murphy was a friend and classmate who on occasion had a lunchtime visit from one of his older brothers, Gerry or Timmy, and the treat of a hot dinner brought to be eaten in their car. I often thought it would be great to have an older brother like Michael's, not for the dinner, but because he had a choice of cars from the Fiat–Lancia garage and filling station their father Jim had across the bridge in Ballyleague. We would tease him about being spoiled and he gave as good as he got. On 18 December 1978, I wasn't surprised to see Gerry arrive at the classroom door and guessed Michael was going to benefit from an early lunch. Yet the headmaster returned and advised Michael to gather his possessions and prepare to leave with his brother.

Waiting a minute and double-checking to make sure they had indeed left, the headmaster announced that Pat Murphy, Michael's 19-year-old brother, had been shot dead in Dublin. As we sat in silence, stunned and saddened for the entire Murphy family, the prayers once again being recited for a young man taken far too young from this life, my head filled with thoughts, questions and no small amount of fear about this notion of death that was creeping ever closer.

Earlier in that summer of 1978, Argentina won the FIFA World Cup and Mario Kempes was the star player we all wanted to be. In my mind I was Kempes, scoring the winning goals (in reality just kicking a ball against the gable of our house), when my attention was drawn to the sound of a car pulling up outside the gateway. I was fascinated with cars and could identify the make and model from different angles and distances, a skill that stood me well later in life as a garda when a glimpse of a suspect vehicle was all I needed. Here, however, was an engine unlike anything I had ever heard before. It was the largest car I had ever laid eyes upon, a shiny, maroon-coloured Rolls-Royce Silver Shadow, which boasted massive wheels finished with mirrored silver hubcaps, with the distinctive RR logo in the centre. The driver in his early thirties looked like a movie star with his Polaroid sunglasses and light-blue short-sleeved shirt. His older companion, walking with a limp and possessing a kindly face, asked 'Is your Pop about?' Jim Fallon and his son John were purchasing my uncle Tommy's nearby house and my father was the keyholder.

The three men spoke together for some time as I gazed enviously at the Rolls, marvelling at the cream leather seats, walnut dashboard and, especially, the silver Spirit of Ecstasy figurine on top of the gleaming radiator grille. The symmetrical double headlights and chrome bumpers just added to the glamour. As they were about to depart, John offered, 'Would you like a spin in it?'

As I took my seat, I could not believe the sheer luxury, and was astonished at the sight of the gear selector mounted on the side of the steering wheel column, like an oversized indicator stalk, and the electric windows in operation. Jim explained that he had a car body garage in England which specialised in luxury motors. He told me all about the 6.7-litre petrol engine which seemed to purr whenever his son John accelerated, the car itself appearing to float an inch over the road such was its elegance and opulence. On an absolute high, I craned my neck, hoping that some friends would see me in the back of the Rolls, but none did. Yet there was a warm glow from the experience, which I relived repeatedly as the months passed, in which I visualised myself as the driver.

Seven short months later, on St Patricks Day 1979, my father answered the phone at home and I knew something was wrong by the way he spoke and the concerned tone of his voice. Putting down the phone receiver, he sat quietly for a moment, 'That was Jim Fallon,' he said, 'John is dead.' He had died suddenly in his sleep at his home in Surrey, England at the tender age of 35. His funeral took place shortly afterwards and John was laid to rest in Rathcline Cemetery where my uncle Ciaran was also interred.

On 8 December 1980, John Lennon was shot dead in New York. His song 'Imagine' played on a constant loop on TV, the black and white video repeated over and over. Sometime afterwards, I was gathering leaves in Jim Fallon's garden when he called me into the sitting room.

'I want to show you something, son,' he said. Carrying a huge scrapbook over to the table, he showed me a photograph of himself and John Lennon, which I looked at in disbelief. Jim knew him?

This musical legend who had just been all over the papers and news as the world grappled to come to terms with his early death just as Jim struggled with his own loss?

He shared how John Lennon had arrived one day at his workshop in Chertsey, Surrey in his matt-black Rolls-Royce asking for a major paint restoration. There was photograph after photograph of Jim and John as the car went through different stages of its stunning transformation until the Rolls-Royce attained its iconic yellow base, and psychedelic artwork, forever to be associated with The Beatles' Sergeant Pepper's Lonely Hearts Club album. (The car is now in storage at the British Columbia Museum in Canada.) It was the same unique yellow as Jim's own Rolls-Royce, which was parked outside with the numberplate bearing the registration 45 MBF, the year of his marriage to his wife Mary Bridget Fallon.

◆

Maureen O'Loughlin lived down the road and her kindly nature ensured that her large back garden was an unofficial playground for us all, the family caravan and boat making it doubly attractive. When her son, my friend Michael, was not at his school desk as usual on 25 May 1979, we were shocked to learn that Maureen had died suddenly aged only 47. As our class prayed for her soul, my mind tried in vain to process just how this lovely lady, so patient and kind to us when visiting, could suddenly be gone and how this God we were praying to could take her from her seven young children who needed her.

◆

The Troubles raged on through the summer of 1979, the assassination of Lord Louis Mountbatten at Mullaghmore, County Sligo, and the Warrenpoint ambush in County Down, a bomb blast that killed 19 British soldiers on the same clear August day, both demanded my father's participation in the subsequent investigations. I saw firearms for the first time when he came home for lunch, having conducted an armed explosives escort not long after Pope John Paul II had visited Ireland. A sleek Walther PPK handgun protruded from his shoulder holster as he sat eating at the table beside me – tea, sandwiches and a compact but deadly Uzi submachine gun taken in from the car remaining continuously in his line of vision. This was the Troubles at our own kitchen table. Even though I would later handle and fire an Uzi submachine gun on the firearms range, my memories always associate any mention of the compact deadly weapon with the unique oily smell as we ate, and of course with the late great John Morley.

From a very young age, and right throughout my childhood, I was persistently exposed to the presence of death. A new decade commenced in 1980 but the death of John Morley cast a shadow over the country. Our own small community was once again touched by tragedy, the roads claiming yet another young casualty, Gerry Hanley. Little could I have imagined back then that my own future would involve policing and crime scene investigation into the very thing I had come to fear yet tried so hard to understand.

As I reflect, I see now that my childhood experiences also brought a very youthful resilience, as each hurdle of sadness was contemplated, and the next faced in turn. I lived in a house with a mother who still lived with her brother's tragic death and a father who spoke about the murders he investigated. I was being exposed regularly to the very thing I feared.

Was my later career choice actually a counterphobic defence? Did I gravitate back to that which I most feared, instead of moving away from it? A deep subconscious attempt to master or control the situation in the hope of overcoming the forgotten anxiety of my childhood?

# CHAPTER 2

# GONE BUT NOT FORGOTTEN

Although it was just ten short years since the murders of John Morley and Henry Byrne when I joined the gardaí in 1990, I held no fear of dying myself in the course of my career in frontline policing. The only inkling of my own mortality came in the context of a personal investigation by the late Gerry Doyle, a classmate from Dublin, during our training at Templemore Garda College.

A natural-born questioner of rules and regulations, Gerry had previously been an electrician and union representative at Cadburys, Coolock. In our second week, his innate sense of injustice was roused by the long queues of garda trainees in the canteen at dinner times while instructors and senior officers were having meals served up to them in a sectioned-off area. Our class had been late to dinner following a physical education session and the lengthy file of some 200 ravenous twenty-somethings trailed back along the cafeteria and out the door.

Gerry surveyed the scene and, swiftly removing his training shoulder-markings, advanced to the upper reaches of the queue. With the newly acquired benefit of anonymity, his true status went unrecognised as he sailed past to sit in the officer and instructor dining area. A riotous roar of laughter rippled along the line as Gerry calmly placed his order with an attending waitress, his older appearance and now unmarked uniform masking his identity as a trainee. He cleverly faced back towards the queue to avoid detection. As the laughter grew louder, the faces of the senior officers present quickly soured and, once the breach was discovered, Gerry was swiftly evicted, though not before polishing off the dinner served up to him. Point made, he let himself be escorted from the inner sanctum and dispatched towards the door with his unique gait and head tilted back, roaring laughing.

Gerry's inquisitive nature likewise led him to the Garda College library after what appeared to the rest of us to be a bland sudden death procedural lecture. From those shelves, he presented us with a forensic pathology book displaying graphic full-colour photographs of violent and accidental deaths taken at police crime scenes across the USA and laughed once again as we recoiled from the reality of what we would soon be facing on the outside. There was no turning back now and we tried to console ourselves that maybe it wouldn't be as bad as depicted in the book.

Little did I realise that those graphic images and crime scene photographs would become all too familiar throughout my frontline policing and crime scene investigation duties. The reality of policing in Dublin presented a contrast to the working lives of most people, outside of those in the emergency services. My childhood fear of death had by now been replaced with a resignation towards the sudden and violent loss of life which had now become part of my own working existence.

Driving up the hill to Rathfarnham Garda Station on the evening of 3 September 1992, I knew I was arriving a bit early. Thursday night shifts were usually busy, and I wanted to report a few minutes before my shift began.

That night, I was assigned to a beat patrol, which meant walking on foot for a couple of hours around the Grange Road and Nutgrove areas, answering calls arising in those locations and giving as many residents as possible the sense of assurance that comes from the presence of a garda in uniform.

The public office in Rathfarnham was a crowded space at the best of times, but just after shift change time it was noisy, bustling and cramped, with gardaí preparing for their night's work, phone calls being answered and made, and the usual in-person callers to the front reception desk. The fading cream-coloured wooden edifice was a closed-in counter with two hatches opening inwards to facilitate face-to-face conversations with callers. It was lined with opaque glass and faced a yellow wall with an old, tiled fireplace centred beside a dated-looking wooden press. As I passed the front desk, the phone rang, and I answered it. A quiet, well-spoken male voice who introduced himself as Frank McCann from 39 Butterfield Avenue asked if Detective Garda Brendan Gallagher was working and said that he needed to speak with him. He disclosed that he was concerned about a mark he had located on the rear door of his home, which was just a ten-minute walk from the garda station. Brendan knew all about the circumstances, he added; it was an ongoing issue. I told the caller that he was not on duty that night and asked if I could help in any way, but he turned down my offer to have a patrol car call up, view the mark and provide assistance, saying he was headed for his workplace at The Cooperage public house in Blessington, County Wicklow. I assured him that I would let Detective Garda Gallagher know he had called, after which he hung up. I left a handwritten note for Brendan asking him to contact Frank McCann, grabbed a radio and went to my locker.

The new patrol jacket had recently been issued, a vast improvement on the previous raincoat and greatcoat used since the foundation of An Garda Síochána, which had been totally unsuited for modern policing. A heavy three-quarter length woollen overcoat with six large shiny gold-effect buttons, the greatcoat resembled those worn by German and Russian army generals during the Second World War.

The new one was lightweight, waterproof and warm, its exterior made of a good quality Gore-Tex material and it looked smart and presentable. Once I had zipped up and attached the reflective Scotchlite belt around my waist with a hoop to hold the Maglite torch, I was set for a good long walk on the beat. I took off down the incline towards the lower-level roadway, turned left and set off towards 39 Butterfield Avenue to see where exactly it was located and whether there had been any unusual activity. It seemed curious that the resident there had only found a mark on the rear door, and no noticeable signs of an attempted break-in.

I had just reached the front of Rathfarnham Shopping Centre when my radio crackled with a call to take a look out for a few young lads causing a disturbance at Lower Dodder Road. I diverted and, walking briskly towards the monument on the junction with Dodder Park Road, I came across a group of youths having a few cans of beer. They were pleasant-mannered and doing no great harm, but since there were elderly people living close by, I asked the lads to move on, which they did without any fuss. I continued my beat up around Churchtown and circled back around by Nutgrove

Avenue, eventually returning to the garda station for a break in the company of Sergeant Tony Heavey from Tallaght Garda Station, before making my way to the Russian Embassy on Orwell Road, Rathgar. The next four hours of my shift were to consist of mind-numbing protection-post duty there. Outside the building, I turned my key in the ignition to cut the engine. Hours of tedium awaited.

Exactly two miles away, another driver was turning a car key, holding it too long in position and panicking as the ignition screeched in protest before he sped away from the scene. At that moment, a massive fireball explosion blew out from the front hallway of 39 Butterfield Avenue while Frank McCann's wife Esther and niece Jessica slept upstairs. In a statement made later to gardaí, their neighbour Richard Duggan explained that his bedroom was in the front of the house directly opposite the McCann's. When he heard the loud bang and the sound of breaking glass, he had looked out to see a ball of flames coming from the front door. The first fire officer from Dublin Fire Brigade at the scene described this entry point as being open and the seat of the fire being in the front hall, with the stairway appearing to act as a chimney for the flames. Hearing the call go out on the radio, I was gripped by a tightening, foreboding sensation. Tony Heavey had just arrived at Butterfield Avenue on his way back to Tallaght Station and was looking for assistance. The radio crackled again and I was sent to the scene to assist.

The smell of burning hit me as I passed Rathfarnham Shopping Centre for the second time in a few short hours. At Butterfield Avenue, I was greeted by the sight of two fire tenders, two ambulances and a huddle of neighbours watching on in silent shock. The fire brigade had responded quickly and managed to prevent the large semi-detached house and garage from being fully consumed. They were lightly spraying down small flame traces, which flickered slowly when the water pressure was reduced. Wispy plumes of smoke and steam rose slowly as the indirect spray passed over the pile of fire debris on the front lawn, which had been pulled out of the burning house. The driveway and footpath were wet and covered in black sediment from the fire officer's passage.

Tony Heavey was there with Garda John Reynolds and asked me to take up duty preserving the scene saying, 'It looks like we have at least two confirmed dead. The husband arrived and tried to get into the burning house, so we had to pull him back and he collapsed.' He nodded towards an ambulance parked parallel to a fire engine in front of the driveway. Frank McCann was sitting on the stretcher behind the ambulance apparently hysterical with grief and each time he managed to pull the oxygen mask away from his face he shouted, 'The guards know.' Surveying the scene, I was shocked at the stark sight of a double fatal house fire and the visible distress of the man I had spoken to earlier on the phone. This was cruel reality and I interrogated myself internally. Why had I not ignored the call about some lads who were doing no harm and taken a look at the house instead?

The next few hours passed in a haze as I stared for ages at the charred front hallway and stairway leading to the landing and bedroom where Esther and Jessica lay, unable to bring myself to shine my torch into the darkness. At one stage Mae Warner, an elegant-looking elderly woman standing in the garden of a neighbouring house, began to cry. Tears flowed down her kindly face, which somehow still radiated a special calmness.

It was 4:00 a.m. before the chaos surrounding the scene started to subside and Andrew Ralph from An Bord Gáis approached to ensure that the mains to the house was off so that there would be no further risk to public safety. I stood there as he checked the supply feed and diligently registered his presence in my notebook. Numbed, though not from boredom, I remained preserving the scene until 6:40 a.m. when I was finally relieved from my duty.

Driving back to my shared accommodation, I knew that sleep would not come and there was no point in going to bed. Instead, I sat in an eerie silence, immersed in a constant replay of the previous night's events. My housemates had gone home for the weekend, and I was alone with a constant feeling of sadness, with no great appetite for my next shift, which was due to begin at 10.00 p.m. It was a typical Friday night as I started the shift, busy with calls stacked up and left over from earlier. Other than a brief discussion at parade time about who would be preserving the scene, there was little talk of the fatal fire or no one even said anything to hint that they knew of the burden I was carrying. That evening was a standard roster – attending to domestic violence incidents, drunkenness, assaults, public order offences and gangs of youngsters huddling in groups bringing neighbourhood attention on themselves. I was exhausted from lack of sleep and the tragedy was weighing heavily on me by the time the shift ended at 6:00 a.m. It was the start of a couple of days off, all of which I spent teasing out every alternative outcome if I had only advanced just a short distance further to Butterfield Avenue. No matter which scenario I conjured up though, I couldn't shake the uneasy feeling from my core.

Unbeknownst to me, however, the days in between had seen numerous case conferences at Rathfarnham and Tallaght Garda Stations. A different picture was slowly emerging of events in the weeks and months before the fire, and the image of Frank McCann as heartbroken hero and husband was slowly starting to unravel. On my return to work, Detective Garda Brendan Gallagher waved the handwritten note and envelope I had left for him. Immaculately dressed as ever, he was wearing a light brown check sports jacket, a pale-blue shirt, a stylish paisley tie, brown pants and complementary polished brown shoes. One of nature's gentlemen, a veteran detective of over 30 years' service and somebody who had seen it all before, nothing flustered Brendan.

'Come on upstairs, we need to have a chat.'

I braced myself, wondering what was to follow. The detective branch office was empty, and he sat down behind an old-style desk, wooden rimmed with a green laminate top.

'I want a statement from you,' Brendan said, turning the note towards me. 'This will form an important part of a chain of evidence presented at the murder trial.'

I was utterly confused. 'But why would a note about a call from a grieving husband be relevant?'

'Ah,' sighed Brendan, 'when you've been around as long as I have, nothing is ever as it seems.'

I sat in silence, reflecting on the cryptic comment, my face surely revealing the sadness I held inside.

'Are you okay?' he enquired, after looked at me for what seemed like an age.

'Not really, Brendan, the whole thing is upsetting me.'

He looked at me incredulously as I recounted the sequence of events, starting with taking the phone call from Frank McCann, leaving the note for Brendan and then the fateful diversion just a few minutes away from taking a look at the house.

'Ah, not at all, young lad,' he said in a kindly voice. 'Don't be worrying. This was 10:00 p.m. and what were you going to do, hide in the garden for another three hours until the fire started, was it?'

'I suppose,' I spluttered unconvincingly.

Speaking in a hushed tone, he went on. 'Listen to me now very carefully, you are not to breathe a word of this to a soul or it could jeopardise the entire investigation.'

I nodded in agreement. He explained that the call I had taken that fateful night was but the last in a sequence that Frank McCann had placed of late to both Blessington and Rathfarnham Garda Stations. There had also been a number of incidents at 39 Butterfield Avenue, including a major gas leak on 28 July 1992, which released a significant level of toxic fumes into the house. Esther had barely managed to escape with Jessica in her arms without igniting the place. It was the investigation team's view that Frank had been trying to establish a series of false threats to harm him, with arson the recurring theme.

On 13 August 1992, Frank McCann had called to Rathfarnham Garda Station and told Garda Eamon Sweeney he had received threatening calls to his home, despite his telephone number being ex-directory, and claimed that his wife was upset by them. That same day he reported to Sergeant Martin Walker and Sergeant Patsy Glennon at Blessington Garda Station that two weeks previously he had received an anonymous call at his public house, The Cooperage, asking whether it was well-insured. He also alleged getting a similar call to his home the previous day from a male caller who impressed on him the importance of being insured. Less than two weeks later, on 25 August 1992, Frank McCann again called to Blessington Garda Station and told Sergeant Patsy Glennon that he had received a call at The Cooperage at 12:15 a.m. the previous night saying, 'I know you have been up to the boys,' by which he understood to mean the gardaí. He claimed the caller had gone on to say, 'You and the fucker across the road are in for it now.'

He took this threat as referring to Tim Grace, a fellow publican whose premises was indeed across the road from The Cooperage and who it transpired was also receiving threatening telephone calls. The investigation was focusing on the possibility that Frank McCann had made these decoy-threatening calls so as to involve another publican as well as himself. And as if to leave no final doubt about intimidation from an unidentified source, he had phoned the gardaí at Blessington Station a few days later on 31 August 1992 and reported that the wall of his licensed premises had been daubed with paint, 'Burn, You Bastard.'

Relief washed over me in waves as I sat there in stunned silence feeling somewhat better that this wise, senior detective had confided such sensitive information in me about the investigation. It was shocking to now hear that Frank McCann was being actively investigated as the prime suspect in the premeditated murders of Esther and Jessica. How could this man who presented as a pillar of the community to the outside world possess such a cold and calculating nature? His physical presence screamed ordinary, decent, hardworking man, which he surely was, successful in both business enterprises and pastimes. Chairman of the Leinster branch of the Irish Amateur Swimming Association and a former international champion swimmer, everything about him exuded respectability.

Yet, unknown to his wife Esther, Frank McCann had breached his position of trust and fathered a child with one of his underage swimming students, a 17-year-old girl with special needs. Learning of Frank and Esther's application in May 1991 to adopt the biological daughter of Frank's sister Jeannette, the student's family lodged an objection with the Adoption Board, who decided to look deeper into it. Only Frank had been notified by their family solicitor of the Adoption Board's decision to reject the couple's application and the likelihood of exposure was now greater than ever. Esther, entirely unaware of this and fed up with the delay and stonewalling for what should have been the most straightforward of cases, scheduled a meeting of her own with the Adoption Board on Monday 7 September 1992. (Cruelly, that turned out to be the day of her and Jessica's removal to Our Lady's Church of Mount Carmel, Firhouse.)

Fact by irrefutable fact, the investigation team became aware of Frank's shadowy web of deceit. It grew clear that he had been fabricating an elaborate sequence of reports about threats received, many involving the theme of burning, with a pattern and level of premeditation barely imaginable and ultimately leading back to himself. Soon the time would come to arrest and detain him. While preserving the scene at 39 Butterfield Avenue many times during the week following the fire, I was fascinated by the work of the crime scene investigators from the Garda Technical Bureau – the methodical way they worked and the intensity with which they conducted their examination. Little did I know then that tiny seeds were being sown for a future career specialisation.

I was present on the morning of 11 September 1992 when the crime scene examinations had been completed and Sergeant Tony Heavey officially handed back the scene at 39 Butterfield Avenue to Frank McCann. Watching very closely as he looked at the awful sight of his house, a wistful, faraway look on his face, I wondered if he had any inkling of the case being methodically pieced together against him. The forensic team had evidence that the fire had been started by an explosion of a gas cannister in the hallway of 39 Butterfield Avenue. Moreover, the technician who carried out the repair of the highly unusual gas leak on 28 July 1992, originating at an access point inside the house which had been tampered with, had attached an extra fitting on the pipe connection to ensure that it could not happen again. Investigations by the Garda Technical Bureau and An Bord Gáis conclusively established that not only had this extra fitting been manipulated but that it could only have been done by somebody with the technical knowledge to apply heat to the seal. Both logically and forensically, it was inconceivable that a random burglar had broken into the house, located the gas access point and possessed the tools and technical know-how to tamper with the pipe collar added as an extra precaution.

A witness statement confirming the explosion and a successful simulation using the same materials found at the scene formed the basis for Frank McCann's arrest on 4 November 1992 under Section 30, Offences Against the State Act. This allowed for a

48-hour detention period, compared with the standard 12 hour maximum under Section 4 of the Criminal Justice Act, a decision unsuccessfully contested at trial by Mr Barry White SC.

Two days later, on 6 November 1992, Frank McCann made a partial confession. However, halfway through his statement of admission in the presence of his solicitor, he was informed that his period of detention had expired, and he was free to leave. He did so, but then returned a couple of minutes later, his solicitor still present, and recommenced the confession with the same parties present in the room, an event which later formed grounds for an application to the trial judge for this statement to be withheld from the jury. Fortunately, the Court of Criminal Appeal held in March 1998 that the confession had been correctly admitted into evidence by the trial judge. On 22 April 1993, Frank McCann was arrested in Waterford and charged with the murders of Esther and Jessica. His first trial commenced on 11 January 1994 and fell apart 20 days later when he tried to set fire to himself with a gas lighter using deodorant as an accelerant in a toilet at Arbour Hill Prison.

It was 10 June 1996 before a second trial got under way, this time presided over by Mr Justice Paul Carney, a gruff, curmudgeonly figure who glowered down from the bench issuing rebukes to witnesses, gardaí, counsel and often the gathered crowd of onlookers. The large attendance seemed to irritate him, with every seat taken and an overflow of people standing. His blood would slowly start to boil with the hum of chatter from the public seats, to which he frequently issued stern warnings and threats of contempt of court. But his brilliant legal mind and powers of retention were evident from the start. Although sometimes cutting in his delivery, his manner displayed perceptive assessments of witnesses. This was particularly noticeable during the *voir dire* or 'trial within a trial', in which legal arguments were teased out on the admissibility of evidence in the absence of the jury.

The defence team cross-examined selected prosecution witnesses that they were trying to have excluded, before making a lengthy submission as to why their testimony should not go in front of the jury. Mr Justice Carney often appeared not to be listening, eyes wandering disinterestedly around the courtroom, when he was in fact absorbing every minute detail of what was said. He would then rise to consider the submissions before returning to give his judgment regarding admissibility. Until giving evidence myself, I had not realised what an amazing ability he had to write while taking in his surroundings, keeping detailed notes in a large A4 hardback journal, which enabled him to quote verbatim from witness testimony.

Mr Justice Carney laid great emphasis on the tone, demeanour and delivery of the witness, then delivered his judgments in a matter-of-fact way. He cut an intimidating figure walking around the Four Courts, wig fixed, gown trailing, a seemingly stern look on his bespectacled face, an unusual, portly gait accentuated by his short steps behind the tipstaff paving their way through the crowded passageways. He had a presence as he passed and knew it; everybody gave him a wide berth.

The trial itself was tense and action-packed, with apparently irrefutable testimony from prosecution witnesses being methodically picked apart by the probing questions of the defence barrister, Mr Barry White SC. He was like a shark sniffing the scent of blood whenever an inconsistency in witness testimony presented. He reserved an even more detailed layer of questioning for the garda witnesses and would meticulously unravel any loose thread in their testimony. When in full flow, a metaphorical kill in his sights, he would theatrically turn around, place one foot on his seat and sweep his gown behind him in preparation for the onslaught. Then he would deliver a searing, withering cross-examination, his dramatic, disdainful gaze picking out somebody in the body of the court as his razor-sharp legal mind prepared his next barb. Now suddenly his focused attention would return to glare at the witness just in time to drive home the import of his question. Although small in physical stature, his professional brilliance loomed large over the proceedings.

It was an education to watch him in action, a frightening and yet enlightening experience, knowing that my time would soon come to face his ferocious scrutiny. I prepared myself for a searching cross-examination, deep-lying memories of my initial worries bubbling close to the surface, but my evidence went uncontested.

For me the key witness was Sergeant Patsy Glennon from Blessington Garda Station, whose evidence was critical in building a clear picture for the jury of Frank McCann's mindset. Slowly, deliberately and methodically, he gave his testimony in a most impressive fashion. I will never forget the sight of him producing the old-style occurrence book from Blessington Garda Station, each page A3 in size, in which matters reported to the gardaí were handwritten along with the subsequent action taken, which was entered on the opposite page.

For all the value of the PULSE computer system, which was developed later, it was hard to beat this book for practicality, effectiveness and instant visibility on taking up duty. The first time I had ever heard the term 'contemporaneous notes' was when Mr Justice Carney had a robust exchange with Mr White SC regarding his objection to the prosecution's introduction of the occurrence book.

Sergeant Patsy Glennon had detailed notes of every report Frank McCann had made about the threats being levelled against him, and Mr Justice Carney was categorical about the value he placed on these entries. Patsy exuded a quiet and efficient confidence as he recounted contact after contact with Frank McCann, each detailed meticulously in his own notes or those of the occurrence book. Frank McNally, covering the trial for the *Irish Times*, 17 August 1996, was similarly impressed:

> He had invited Sgt Patsy Glennon to his house for a quiet chat but the Garda later made a very detailed memorandum of the four-hour conversation, which gave important clues on the way McCann was thinking. Sgt Glennon, whose affable and easy-going exterior belied his efficiency, came in for special treatment from the defence during the trial, in which he was branded a 'wolf in sheep's clothing'.

It was little wonder that Sergeant Glennon drew such attention from the defence. Had they somehow been able to discredit his evidence, it could have been detrimental to the prosecution case. But his testimony survived scrutiny and he himself was called to the Bar 22 years later.

Day after long day in the roasting courtroom, witness after witness was called, testimony asserted and then tested robustly by the defence team. It was impossible to know how the trial was progressing. The jury members were impassive throughout the 48 days, one of the longest-running trials in Irish legal history. On day 39, the atmosphere was tense in advance of the arrival of Mr Justice Carney. A scramble for seats had commenced early, regular attendees unimpressed that their regular spots were under siege. Today was different: Frank McCann was to take the witness stand in his own defence.

The air in the courtroom bristled with what seemed like an electrical charge as I sat there taking in the overhead public gallery packed to capacity. I looked up at the raised judge's bench, a big leather chair carrying the imposing outline of Mr Justice Carney in his wing collar, jabot and gown, horsehair wig perched on his head, impassively peering over his spectacles at the scene below. Behind the chair hung a huge dark curtain suspended from an oversized, varnished wooden canopy. A large gold harp was affixed to the wall above that, symbolising justice and the Irish State. It was surrounded by a semicircular decorative plaster detail and above that the ceiling was rimmed with the most ornate plaster work extending around in symmetrical opposite directions. A large rectangular light-filled atrium spilled daylight down into the courtroom, a James Gandon architectural marvel dating back to 1796. The registrar was at a desk lower than Mr Justice Carney's bench. To one side was the registrar's assistant and on the other the stenographer, hands poised to record the transcript. On the next level was the defence solicitor, and the State solicitor. Facing them on one side was Mr Barry White SC, assisted by Mr Anthony Sammon BL and Mr Kenneth Mills SC assisted by Mr Tom O Connell BL for the prosecution.

'Mr Frank McCann,' called out Mr Barry White, as he motioned him towards the witness box. The packed courtroom fell silent. All eyes were on the accused as he rose slowly from his seat, his expression neutral, and walked the short distance to the witness box before swearing to almighty God that he would tell the truth, the whole truth and nothing but the truth. He sat silently in the witness box, shoulders slightly forward and rounded, waiting for Mr White to begin leading him through his evidence. Wearing a dark pullover over a white shirt, tie and grey pants, his glasses seemed oversized and his brown hair was neatly groomed with a side parting, his pale and smooth face betraying no sign of emotion. He was the picture of conservative ordinariness, giving the same initial impression of decency and propriety when I first saw him; this was probably also the case for many others in the courtroom. I wondered what the jury were thinking, unaware as they were that Frank McCann had been in custody since being charged. He was outwardly calm and assured as he spoke, Barry White leading him with some introductory prompts. His voice was deeper than I had remembered, but a change seemed to come over him as he proceeded. I noticed a slight quiver in his voice and then he stopped talking.

Judge Carney peered down, watching closely as Frank McCann started shivering, then shaking. He began taking deeper and deeper gulps of air, holding onto the witness box as if to steady himself and appearing to be having some type of seizure or panic attack. His glasses were moving closer to the end of his nose and seemed ready to fall off as he shook more violently, hyperventilating. The courtroom was transfixed by the scene playing out, the jury likewise absorbing every detail.

36

This wasn't the first time that Frank had behaved this way. It was a pattern which had developed whenever he was under pressure, as if his efforts to stay composed would desert him and the enormity of the situation took him over. It happened at the scene of the fire, it happened when he was in garda custody, it happened when he was being questioned as the trail he had laid was starting to lead back towards himself, and it was happening again now. As I glanced across at Marian Leonard, Esther's sister, I noticed she wore a resigned look, as if knowing this to be a ploy to delay proceedings. Judge Carney rose and allowed for medical attention as Frank McCann's legal team assisted him from the witness box, before later adjourning until the following Tuesday.

Eventually, the end of the trial edged closer and the jury prepared to consider the weeks of evidence they had heard. Was it enough to convict Frank McCann or would he walk from the Central Criminal Court a free man? It was delicately poised as Barry White delivered a compelling closing speech on behalf of the defence. Absorbing every minute detail during the trial, I was fascinated by the cut and thrust of the exchanges. I learned that detailed investigation, meticulous note-taking, and confident, measured delivery of evidence in the witness box was more than a match for the most robust of cross-examinations. It was evenly balanced, and the courtroom bristled with tension.

Mr Justice Paul Carney then made his charge to the jury, summarising the evidence they had heard and reminding them that they must acquit Frank McCann of the charges he faced if they had even the slightest doubt about his guilt. They were sent away to deliberate on their verdict and returned late that evening to say that they had not yet reached one. Marian Leonard described the tension: 'It was unbearable, the thought kept recycling in my mind that the jury were having difficulty with their decision.' They were sent to a hotel room for the night and resumed their deliberations the following morning, continuing right throughout the forty-eighth day.

At 6:20 p.m., just when it seemed things could not get any more tense, the six men and six women of the jury returned to the courtroom and told Mr Justice Carney that they could not reach a unanimous verdict. There was a suspicion that, while convinced of Frank McCann's intent to murder Esther, some were concerned about his alleged affection for baby Jessica. Mr Justice Carney then directed that he would accept a majority verdict of 10-2 or 11-1. Finally, at 6:45 p.m., word filtered through that they were returning.

'Have you reached a verdict?' Mr Justice Carney asked.

'We have,' replied the foreman of the jury.

'On the counts of the murder of Esther McCann and Jessica McCann, how do you find the accused, guilty or not guilty?'

The foreman paused for what seemed like an age, as if considering for one final time the enormity of what he was about to say, took a deep breath and then spoke.

'Guilty on both counts.'

As the courtroom erupted into shouts, tears and joy at the verdict, Frank McCann stared straight ahead impassively, betraying no emotion as Judge Carney sentenced him to two life sentences, which were to run concurrently, and refusing leave to appeal.

The verdicts ended a nine-week trial and an investigation lasting four years but without an end to the pain and sorrow for Esther's family. As her 83-year-old mother, Mrs Bridget O'Brien, said afterwards, 'He could have taken Esther into his confidence and he'd have found her very understanding. But he was too proud and it wouldn't have done his image in the swimming world to have a scandal like that. So he killed his two best friends, his only friends. The people who would have stood by him no matter what happened.'

———◆———

Thirty-one years after the shocking deaths of Jessica and Esther, they were on my mind again. I had come across a newspaper article recounting the case and the fact that Frank McCann had withdrawn his sixth application for parole. Esther's sister Marian was quoted in the newspaper piece and I subsequently listened to a podcast interview with her and her own daughter Esther. I decided to reach out to Marian and was delighted when she responded.

On 12 December 2023 I was greeted by her warm, friendly face and piercing blue eyes as we got to speak in person for the first time since the trial all those years before. Marian shared insights into Esther's fun-loving personality, her kindness, and her deep love for little Jessica. Marian generously consented to the final words of this chapter being from Esther's poignant diary salvaged by garda technical experts from the ruins of her fire-damaged computer:

30 July 1992 – My darling daughter Jessica, you have grown and become a beautiful child. You have been walking now for a little over a week and have given up holding onto the walls in search of your own bit of independence. 'Cup of tea' and 'Up a daisy' with constant talk of 'Daddy', 'Oh Mammy' and

'Mammy's baby'. Lots of talk and every day brings new joys of every sort in sight, sound, speech and movement.

Ten teeth to show for all the months of painful teething which gave you such problems with infections of all sorts. Nana's little darling in everything you do, she never ceases to love looking at you and you can really amaze with your antics, including playing the piano with much style and seriousness. May next door will have to take you for lessons soon. The hottest and driest summer in years.

# CHAPTER 3

# DEATH OF INNOCENCE

Although Rathfarnham was quieter than my first training station Blanchardstown, it covered an extensive geographical area and was in the same 'M' garda district as Tallaght, by far the busiest station in the Dublin Metropolitan Area South. Initial exposure to regular accidental and sudden deaths was soon followed by murder scenes, which provided a basis for my later role in crime scene investigation. The 1992 murders of Esther and Jessica, barely a mile down the road from Rathfarnham Garda Station, had brought home the stark reality of city policing.

That wasn't the last time I was exposed to the cruelty of a double murder. On 24 November 1995, I had just attended a call in Tallaght and was heading back towards Rathfarnham station at 5:00 a.m., an hour before my shift was due to end, when I could go home to sleep while the rest of the city got up to go to work. The radio crackled to life with a report of gunshots fired on Cheeverstown Road, just a few minutes away from where I was. Immediately a follow-up message reported that there was a man lying on the road. Approaching the stretch of roadway near Whitebrook housing estate, I could see the flashing blue lights of the Tallaght patrol car coming from the other direction and, even closer ahead, a stationary Nissan Micra with its lights on and passenger door open. Even at this relatively early stage of my service, I knew the vital importance of first attenders at serious incidents. In the midst of even the most shocking scenes, calmness, quiet observation and a detailed memory were an absolute must. I had witnessed how the smallest of details might yet assume the greatest relevance at a later trial. A seemingly innocuous or mistaken recollection could be used to give the defending counsel an opportunity to cast a doubt on witness testimony. As I slowed, I reminded myself how everything I saw and did could be crucial at a later stage.

I swung the patrol car across the roadway to act as a barrier twenty yards short of the Micra, as a Tallaght patrol car had already done on the far side. Then I ran towards the motionless body of a male lying on the roadway three feet or so behind the Nissan Micra, Garda Louise Hickey standing close by, having arrived just before me. A round bullet hole was clearly visible on the side of his forehead and a small pool of blood was forming on the roadway. Dressed casually in a tracksuit and Asics runners, with his left knee raised as if he was about to get up, only the small wound indicated the gravity of his situation. While Louise checked for vital signs, my attention was drawn to the open door of the Nissan Micra.

The body of a female passenger leaned outward and downward, her legs still inside the car and her feet in the footwell. She was being suspended by the safety belt, which had extended to hold her shoulder and head, just 18 inches from the ground. A large pool of blood had formed on the roadside, the blood coming from the bullet wound on her head. It looked like the car had been flagged down, the open driver's window suggesting an initial exchange before the fatal shootings.

The Micra's automatic transmission was in the park position, an interior light illuminating the scene, the car key in the ignition and a keyring with the name Linda still rotating slowly. A packet of John

Player Blue cigarettes lay on top of a cushion on the driver's seat as a Minnie Mouse figurine watched on impassively from the dashboard, the familiar wide-eyed look seemingly alarmed at the sight below. A smouldering cigarette sat on the lip of the ashtray, signs of normal life just moments earlier. I leaned over and whispered a small prayer for the woman's soul, knowing she was gone.

The immediate first few minutes with just a few colleagues present at such a scene was the calm before the storm of activity about to be unleashed. There was a sense of death in the air and shock at the cruel reality of it all. As the road filled up with assisting personnel, I stood there calmly writing up my notes, knowing that every detail could be relevant. The streetlight, I noticed, was reflected in the thick dark pool of blood, and that, along with the orange-tinted hue, flashing blue strobe lights and personnel giving radio updates, it was not unlike a scene from a movie. Even at that early hour, a handful of onlookers had started to gather.

Back on the verge, I scanned for discarded shell casings. Then, stepping back a little further, I took out a black, non-fade felt pen and sketched the Nissan Micra with its lights still on, passenger door open, window shattered and former occupants now lifeless. The scrawly simplicity of my sketch depicting the position of the bodies looked so plain compared with the actual roadside death scene I stood at.

Dr James Moloney arrived a few minutes later and pronounced both victims dead. Outside the crime scene tape, arriving detectives conferred on the next procedural step in the murder investigation and looked on at the awful reality of this early November morning. Motive, circumstance, opportunity, the last person to see both alive were all issues for deep enquiry, but that was for the first murder conference a few short hours later. (This is a conference chaired by a detective superintendent and attended by investigating gardaí for the purposes of assigning tasks and directing avenues of investigation.)

The victims were quickly identified as 30-year-old father-of-four Eddie McCabe from Glenshane Park, Tallaght, and his passenger, 28-year-old mother-of-two Catherine Brennan of Knockmore Crescent. This was a double assassination, and it was all the more vicious for the merciless manner with which Catherine Brennan had been executed; the fact she was a potential witness was the only apparent reason for her death. Various theories circulated at the time of the murder, many hurtful to the families of the victims, and while a number of arrests were made during the course of the investigation, not enough evidence was secured to bring the perpetrator to justice. Ultimately, six innocent children were left behind and, for both families concerned, the tragedy did not end there.

Eddie McCabe Junior was only 10 years of age when his dad was murdered. The killing affected him deeply throughout his teenage years. Problems at school and addiction issues followed him closely. Eleven years after his father's death, Eddie Junior was himself the victim of a savage attack, which left him lifeless on a south Dublin roadway too, this time just off Tyrconnell Road, Inchicore. Catherine Brennan's sister Noeleen was likewise brutally murdered in her home, just a short distance from where Catherine had been executed 15 years' earlier. Like Eddie Junior, Noeleen had never fully recovered from the events of 24 November 1995 and also struggled with addiction issues up until her time of death.

———◆———

Fifteen months later, murder returned to the environs of Rathfarnham Garda Station and once more I was present to experience the aftermath. Franco Sacco was a local businessman running Luigi's takeaway restaurant on Main Street, Rathfarnham village. He cut a familiar figure around the local area, with jet-black tightly cropped hair, a strong stocky build and dark piercing eyes. He was every inch the hardworking Italian, with a keen interest in football, cars and hunting. He had a red sporty VW Golf that was immaculately maintained and always parked close to the restaurant.

Franco was a friendly, outgoing figure behind the counter and, along with his youthful wife Anna Maria, served his customers with a smile and some small talk. He would often wear an Inter Milan replica jersey, its distinctive blue and black stripes signalling his loyalties, a plain gold rope necklace always visible over the jersey. Many times, while waiting for my order, we chatted about the Italian Serie A, at the time the strongest football league in the world.

The day of 20 March 1997 was relatively quiet policing-wise in the 'M' district, at least to begin with. Following an overtime drugs patrol, I had returned to the garda station at 7:30 p.m. and was in the sergeant's office, having just signed my radio back in, when the sound of screaming came from the public office. Garda Ronan Waldron had brought a hysterical 14-year-old Vicki Whelan in, who he was trying to calm down.

'She claims that she's shot Franco Sacco dead,' said Ronan.

I could barely believe what I was hearing. 'Where?' I asked, and she blurted out the location between anguished roars.

From his distinctive red VW Golf, I knew Franco's house

was at 3 Coolamber Park, Templeogue. I grabbed the keys to an unmarked patrol car and, joined by Garda Garrett Billings, raced the short few minutes' drive there. We found Franco's car parked in the driveway, the house in darkness and a locked front door. From the outside, there were no signs of anything amiss.

Soon we were joined by Sergeant Johnny Byrne, who had located the key to the front door, and Garda Jim Murphy. The house seemed so still as I popped on a latex glove, flicked on the hall and landing lights, and trailed Johnny up the stairs, Jim following. Each step up the stairs seemed to magnify the silence as we climbed.

Johnny slowly opened the master bedroom door. On the bed before us, a large bloodstain covered the top of the bare mattress. The wall above it was stained by wipe marks – a clear sign of an attempted cleanup. And beside the bed, on the floor, lay what was clearly a body, wrapped in sheets, blankets and bed clothes. Tentatively, Johnny carefully peeled back two outer blankets, an electric blanket, then bloodstained towels and sheets. Every layer he carefully stripped away until the body was revealed.

'Is it him?' he asked.

I looked down at the familiar head of cropped black hair, now matted with blood from a shotgun blast.

'It's definitely Franco,' the shock still not quite fully registering.

Johnny replaced the covers, and we immediately withdrew from the murder scene, the preservation of which was of the utmost importance. Taking a quick look in the bathroom, I saw what looked like a tiny piece of clotted blood in the sink, the bloody mark still visible. A black plastic bin liner sat on the landing with cleaning materials observable through the opening.

Outside, a crowd had already gathered. The driveway was sealed off now with the familiar 'Crime Scene Do Not Enter' tape forming a barrier to the property.

Having attended several murder trials by this point, I knew the vital importance of preserving the scene properly. As we filed out the front door, I noticed that the key was still in the lock. Pulling the door closed behind me, I made sure it was secure before removing the key and placing it in my pocket. Soon the flanks of senior officers would arrive, all wanting to have a look at the scene. From what I had witnessed firsthand in other cases and observed happening at murder trials, I decided that the best thing I could do for this investigation was to keep that key in my trousers pocket. Garrett Billings and I remained there preserving the scene. When Garda Detective Pat Normile arrived, I told him I had the key. While it probably did not sit well with some of the senior officers, it was favourably remarked upon by the Garda Technical Bureau crime scene investigation team who arrived the next morning to examine the scene.

It wasn't long before a car pulled up and, as a hush descended on the gathered crowd, Anna Maria Sacco stepped out, along with her cousin and friend. She took in the three patrol cars, numerous gardaí and her garden sealed off with crime scene tape.

'What's wrong?' she cried out. 'I was ringing and ringing, and no answer. The chipper was closed and I was wondering what was wrong.'

I brought Anna Maria inside the tape and over to the semi-privacy of the porch area.

'Anna Maria,' said Pat Normile, the senior garda present. 'Franco is dead'.

She charged the front door, banging her head off it, tears streaming down her face.

'He's only asleep,' she kept shouting. 'He's only asleep, he's only asleep.'

Pat led her into the neighbour's house away from the onlookers. It was the second time I had witnessed the distress of a spouse at a murder scene in front of assorted emergency personnel and gathered onlookers. Detective Garda Brendan Gallagher's words of experience and wisdom were in the back of my mind as I made detailed notes of every word and action playing out in front of me. By that stage, the media had arrived, their scanners having alerted them to the murder scene. Events were recorded in notebooks even as they played out. One newspaper reporter squeezed his business card into the hand of one of my young colleagues. Now a leading political correspondent, his sharpness and quick thinking were evident even at that early stage of his career.

The garda investigation revealed many twists and turns, as well as the stunning allegation that Anna Maria had plotted to have her husband killed. Evidence was heard from a barman, Peter Gifford, who testified she had asked him to secure a hitman to kill Franco. Once again, a spouse faced a murder trial but this time without the key protagonist, the defence having argued successfully that 14-year-old Vicki Whelan should have a separate trial. Vicki Whelan had already pleaded guilty to murdering Franco Sacco on 19 June 1998. Mr Barry White SC, the defence counsel, summed up the central flaw in the prosecution case – that the person who pulled the trigger was not on trial as a co-accused – contending the case was like 'Hamlet without the Prince'.

The case was a media sensation with the narrative arc unfolding like a plot from a TV crime series, banner headlines generated day after day from evidence given under oath. The trial collapsed after the jury failed to reach a verdict and a new trial was set for January 1999. This time, though, the prosecution was able to call the teenager who had entered the bedroom while Franco slept, pointed Franco's own shotgun at him and pulled the trigger, killing him instantly. Her evidence that Anna Maria had put her up to killing Franco was robustly challenged and the prosecution argued that it was impossible that the teenager could have acted alone without help. Anna Maria Sacco was acquitted of Franco's murder and left the court an innocent woman, free to put her life back together. The young girl Vicki Whelan served a year in custody of her seven-year sentence before being released with the Court of Criminal Appeal adjudging that 'there was no suitable place in the country to detain the young woman.'

Franco is still dead.

By then I had encountered death many times, in all of its manifestations: sudden, accidental and, most of all, deliberate. I was competent in procedural and policing matters concerning fatalities, yet while carrying out my duties, another part of me regularly paused for enquiry into this fate that awaits us all. Regularly recalling my childhood fears, I wondered whether some part of me had divined what lay ahead in my future working life. During that time I would find myself reflecting on those earlier deaths, and when this happened I accepted those revived memories as part of the job; it seemed unavoidable that they would be recalled. Being a garda in 1990s Dublin meant continuous exposure to such violent incidents, as well as an inevitable sadness on witnessing the suffering of grieving families. During those nine years, I attended more murder scenes than most would encounter throughout their full service. It was a time for learning as well as reflection.

Although still a uniformed garda and not a senior investigator, I acquired a comprehensive overview of what a proper detailed investigation should entail.

An early experience I had while protecting a murder suspect patient at St James Hospital Dublin served me well. He had sustained a severe hand injury in the midst of carrying out a fatal stabbing and there were credible threats against him. I was one of two assigned to ensure his safety throughout the night. In the company of highly experienced Garda Kieran Kinsella, I looked on as the suspect began to speak about the stabbing.

Kieran immediately cautioned him.

'You are not obliged to say anything,' he said. 'But anything you do say will be taken down in writing and may be given in evidence.'

The suspect indicated that he understood and continued to express remorse for events as they had happened. Kieran wrote down everything he was saying before reading over the notes of his account and asking me to countersign his notebook, which subsequently resulted in my role as a key witness in the prosecution's case, Kieran being unavailable to give evidence due to his placement in Cambodia on a UN peacekeeping mission. The suspect's admissions were accepted into evidence after I gave my direct evidence, and I was subjected to a relatively mild cross-examination. Once again, I had given evidence at a murder trial, withstanding scrutiny from judge, jury and defence counsel.

My conclusion from attending these various murder trials was that there is only one way to prevent disaster in the witness box: prepare thoroughly for each appearance. I also always ensured that I was immaculately turned out and, when my name was called by the prosecuting counsel, I would stride confidently up to the witness box and stand tall. I made a point of delivering the oath in a loud confident tone, sending a signal to the judge, jury and defence counsel that, although I was a young garda, I would be a competent witness.

As I was giving my evidence I would always lean across midstream, reach for the provided water decanter, pour a glass of water and take a sip without missing a beat. Having seen so many senior officers taken apart in the witness box, I was determined that I would never allow myself to be embarrassed at trial. I always felt that if senior counsels could command the courtroom with the impressive delivery of their cross-examinations, then I too should ensure that my replies were equally confident. This skill could only be acquired by practice, and my early years absorbing the lessons of these high-profile murder investigations was an amazing training ground for my later career as a crime scene investigator.

It was many years later, as my time in Rathfarnham approached its end, that an admission of a fatal knife stabbing again crossed my ears. This time it was made directly to myself. I took notes of what was said.

The 2:00 p.m. to 10:00 p.m. shift in the Rathfarnham patrol

car had been relatively quiet on the night of 8 August 1998. Accompanied by Garda Paul Godson, we were just about to finish up when the radio crackled to life.

'Control to Mike Bravo One, reports coming in of a fatal stabbing at Carrickmount Drive, Rathfarnham.'

Half a minute later, we were pulling up outside the house in question, blocking the driveway with the patrol car. Paul placed crime scene tape across the gateway. Then we made our way to the front door, which was slightly ajar. Just inside it, two Dublin Fire Brigade ambulance personnel were working on the body of a male prone on the hallway floor.

'No chance,' said one of them, starting to gather up their equipment. As I looked up the staircase, I noticed a number of steps were bloodstained.

Opening the door to the kitchen, I took details from those present, before asking what had happened.

'I just came back to drop young Peter home,' said Deborah MacDonald, one of the two women who were there. 'I had been babysitting him all day and I was met by my sister Caroline crying. She told me that [her husband] Peter was dead, and she couldn't wake him, that she'd stabbed him. I told her to get the knife, my partner rang the ambulance, and I stayed here with her until you came.'

At this stage I needed to clear the house and get a proper account of what had occurred. It was always important to take precise details from a suspect at the murder scene, as they could become relevant later were a story to be changed.

The dead man was Peter Comerford, and I was conscious that

his seven-year-old son was also in the living room with his young cousin. I asked Deborah's partner to bring the children away while I remained with the two women. Before they did so, I returned to the hallway and covered Peter's body with a Dublin Fire Brigade blanket, then stood across it as Paul led them outside. There was no need for the victim's son to see the large pool of blood now forming beneath his lifeless father. Then I returned to the living room where Caroline recounted the sequence of events, but not before I formally cautioned her in the manner I had witnessed Kieran Kinsella do years beforehand.

They had been drinking all day, she said. Her husband Peter had fallen asleep in the upstairs bedroom. He had been on green methadone and immediately upon waking had become violent with her. Caroline stated that she had stabbed him in self-protection with a kitchen knife she had retrieved from downstairs. I read back her account to her and asked if it was a true representation of what she had said before inviting her to sign it. I figured that her cast-iron admission would pass legal scrutiny and that her signature on my notebook would add to the strength of the words. Her sister Deborah's account corroborated her own, something that I had also taken note of.

After that, I accompanied her as she went upstairs to retrieve a change of clothing; her own needed to be retained for evidential purposes. When that was done, there was a poignant moment when she cried while stepping across the remains of her husband. When she pointed to where she had stabbed him twice in the legs and once in the back, I took a formal note of it. Then I arranged for her transport in an unmarked car to the garda station, where she would confirm the account she had given me at the scene in a formal statement.

The Director of Public Prosecutions (DPP) concluded that going downstairs and retrieving a knife from the kitchen constituted *mens rea* – guilty intent – which was necessary to warrant a murder charge. As a result, Caroline Comerford was tried for murder in the Central Criminal Court and I was called upon to give detailed evidence. It was here that precise note-taking came into play, allowing me to give evidence of what I had witnessed and heard at the murder scene. Once more my direct evidence underwent the mildest of cross-examinations. I was by now certain that impressive, confident delivery of truthful testimony cut off opportunities for defence counsel to attack. It was truly moving to watch the 15-year-old daughter give evidence that her father was the nicest man you could ever meet and describing how, when her father was drunk, her parents would fight. Ultimately, after two days of deliberations, the jury of seven women and five men delivered a majority not guilty verdict. This case brought it home to me the tragedy that can follow close at hand when alcohol and drugs are in the mix. Susan Comerford, a sister of Peter's, was quoted in the *Sunday Times* on 17 October 2004; she spoke of her sorrow for her brother's loss and her unhappiness with the verdict.

By the late 1990s I had learned to handle the most violent of death scenes in my own unique way, treading softly at first and then later with the confidence of a seasoned professional. Within a decade I would become a crime scene investigator and would train and work closely with the Technical Bureau Garda Headquarters, a team I had watched at close quarters throughout those high-profile cases.

The 1990s was a decade of relentless Dublin gangland killings, On 18 August 1994, Martin Cahill, 'The General', was assassinated in Ranelagh, when he was ambushed in broad daylight, his Renault 5 mounting the footpath with the glass shattered from the gunshots that killed him.

The 1996 cold-blooded execution of *Sunday Independent* crime journalist Veronica Guerin was the most brazen and callous attack on democracy. The State responded by opening the purse strings and establishing the successful Criminal Assets Bureau, its effectiveness resulting in many similar bodies being established across Europe.

When I commenced my policing career in 1990, I was a young lad, aware that I had experienced an unusually high number of deaths in my childhood. By the end of that same decade, I was a married man with a young son, back living in my home town. I was relieved to be away from Dublin, although by the time I became a crime scene investigator, many of the harsh realities of life I had encountered there had spread countrywide. The next decade would see me exposed to mortality on a scale I had never imagined.

# CHAPTER 4

# THE ULTIMATE SACRIFICE

n January 1999, I arrived on transfer to Castlerea Garda Station, where officer-in-charge Sergeant Kevin Bruen gave myself and Garda Colm Horkan a warm welcome, before hinting that management had something special in mind for us. Castlerea Prison had opened in 1996 and, in the autumn before our transfer, a request had been made of management in the Castlerea station for garda personnel to escort remand prisoners to Galway District Court. Prison officers were responsible for escorting those serving prison sentences to and from a circuit or higher court hearing, but this responsibility fell to the gardaí for remand prisoners. This posed a burden on existing station manpower in Castlerea and Colm and I were the solution – a two-man dedicated prison escort unit.

We set about accompanying remand prisoners to district court sittings around the country and whenever there were no escorting duties we worked at the station. After a few weeks this became untenable for us, having no interest in continuously travelling the length and breadth of the country and sitting through long days of court hearings. It also isolated us from our colleagues; we weren't assigned to a working unit or to work weekends or night duty. We sought a meeting with management.

We were apprehensive about having to voice discontent so soon after arriving on transfer. We also both appreciated how fortunate we were to have secured our moves out of Dublin, Colm now but a short trip from home in Charlestown and myself a similar distance from Lanesborough. Superintendent Mick Roche, a friendly outgoing Wexford man, was our boss at the time and he gave us a reasonable hearing. His hands were tied, he explained, in that Garda Headquarters had only sanctioned our transfers on the express grounds that we would be assigned solely to escort duties. The hope was that this approach would lead to a reduction in the ever-escalating overtime bill; the consequences of these new arrangements for transporting remand prisoners on the surrounding operational area, with its skeleton service, had not been taken into account.

Nobody else at the station was especially enamoured with our full-time appointment to this role, as it deprived others with an occasional break from the daily routine of regular policing duties and an opportunity to visit various exotic locales nationwide such as Limerick, Letterkenny, Buncrana, Cavan and Galway. Yet the prospect of this role being our daily reality for the next few years was a mind-numbing prospect for me and Colm. We decided on a wait-and-see strategy, figuring that pressure from our representative body would eventually lead to our 'parole'.

For now, we travelled the length and breadth of the country, experiencing these large towns' different policing workloads firsthand, a sharp contrast from our former city roles. And we saw at close quarters how the administration of justice differed depending on the personality of the judge and the ability of defence solicitors to pick holes in prosecution cases. Sometimes prisoners would be granted bail and on those return trips we would talk about Colm's five years in the K district of Cabra, Finglas and Blanchardstown and my nine in the M district of

Tallaght and Rathfarnham. During these lengthy conversations, I got a strong sense of the decency, integrity and strength of character that comprised the core essence of Colm Horkan. I saw strength of a different kind at close quarters on the football pitch, where his leadership, power and skill on the ball were evident. This was a man you could trust, both on and off the pitch, and even more so in the rough and tumble of frontline policing, where I instinctively knew he would always have your back

The prisoners we transported were generally well-behaved, delighted to be free from the daily monotony of prison life and eager for the prospect of family visits at court. There were rarely any incidents and, as we were not involved in the investigation of the crimes of which they were accused, they would often chat freely about their lives, families and the cases that had landed them in custody. Colm was always kind and humane in his approach, facilitating family visits, food breaks and quick cigarettes whenever possible. It was in our remit to grant such small perks once we did not run the risk of an escape or fights with rival factions in the courthouse.

The wit and intellect of some of these young men elicited a natural sympathy, trapped as they were in a cycle few would ever exit, their lives having unravelled due to a combination of drugs, alcohol and tragic background circumstances. Prison was no deterrent for them, simply part of a way of life, a consequence of the world they lived in. Although most had committed serious crimes – otherwise they wouldn't have been on remand – it was difficult at times to reconcile the entertaining, chatty characters we accompanied with the version of them recounted before the courts.

Before long, our newly formed escort unit was abruptly disbanded when a new block opened at Castlerea Prison, and Colm and I were returned to regular policing duties. We now often found ourselves working on opposite shifts, but we both adjusted to the new reality of country policing.

Castlerea District had not been immune to brutal tragedy, the 1980 murders of John Morley and Henry Byrne at Loughglynn still clear in the living memory of our many new colleagues working on that fateful day. And in 1997, two years before our transfers, serial killer Mark Nash had executed a vicious and sadistic double murder in the quiet village of Ballintober.

On 6 September 2006, during an afternoon shift, I arrested a man for possession of drugs with intent to supply. The prison's arrival to Castlerea had been closely followed by the scourge of drugs arriving there too. Attempts to launch consignments over the high concrete walls of the prison were commonplace. Later in the same shift, I was discussing this with Gardaí Billy Molloy and Tom Cunningham, who had just returned from a prison escort, when the radio crackled with a colleague's voice requesting urgent assistance at a rented house about a mile from the station. The patrol car crew had just responded to a call from someone who was concerned about both their own welfare and that of a family member. On arrival they were greeted by a man swinging a sword and threatening extreme violence if they tried to intervene.

Tom and Billy never shied away from any confrontational encounter, and we all rushed to the bungalow cottage, a small, well-kept building noted for its quaint appearance in front of a builder's supply yard just off the main Ballaghaderreen road on the outskirts of Castlerea. By the time we arrived, there was no one in the small gravel front yard that lay in front of the cottage, its front walls entirely covered with a mature evergreen creeper, windows recessed slightly behind the heavy foliage. The man had retreated back inside with the sword he had been brandishing.

A few onlookers had gathered though, and the patrol car crew briefed us. With no recourse to backup, we discussed our options. Having already confronted him and been threatened by him, it would be better if we tried to resolve the situation and they retreated.

The cottage was subdivided into a number of flats, the man's residence consisting of a living room, kitchenette and bathroom facilities in the right wing of the house. As we spoke, the net curtain of the room to the right of the front door twitched. Tom, Billy and I stepped across the boundary into the gravel drive, just as the front door flew open and the man with the sword, Stephen Silver, emerged.

'Get back to fuck from here,' he roared, his long hair and goatee beard lending to his distinctive presence and aggressive tone. He was tall and very well-built, his muscular arms bulging under the short sleeves of a black t-shirt, a strong pair of boots elevating his height further. Both hands were on the hilt of what appeared to be a samurai-style sword, the curve of the blade clearly visible. There was little doubt that the sword was real, the metallic rasp grating as he flashed it in a quick upwards figure 8 motion, the inside edge momentarily connecting with the concrete plaster door reveal.

We paused our advance and just as quickly as he had appeared, he retreated backwards in a similar martial art style pose, the sword still held outwards. Carefully placing one boot directly behind the other, he darted sideways into the living room, the door slamming behind him.

We moved forward quickly, seizing the opportunity to advance before the front door closed us out and knowing that for the moment we were safely out of the swords range. As we advanced into the hallway, the door to the living area was closed but we could hear Stephen Silver from within, roaring, his voice muffled.

Billy, still outside, went to the front window, where the net curtain had moved earlier.

'Be careful,' he warned, 'he's after putting on a motorbike helmet.'

Tom and I were both fully in the hall now, him on one side of the living room door and me on the other.

'Careful now,' updated Billy, 'he's got the sword again.'

During my 16 years of frontline policing I had managed to escape intact from numerous violent confrontations. I had been threatened with a baseball bat, a hatchet, a Stanley knife, a blood-filled syringe and other items more suited to a toolbox or a kitchen. A long curved razor-sharp samurai sword was a different proposition. There was no textbook answer for dealing with a suspect armed with a deadly sword like this. The general advice for unarmed officers threatened with a bladed weapon comprised four simple words: *Get out of there*. But you can't always follow this advice when you find yourself in a dynamic and volatile confrontation. This situation would depend on a cool-headed approach, we now needed to draw on our intuition, and learned experience of dealing with violent aggressors over a long number of years. This unique siege-type encounter would demand a strategy of calm interaction with Silver and building up a rapport with him.

After a while, the shouting subsided, and Billy indicated that Silver had retreated to the far side of the room. This was not the movies, there was no helmeted, armoured SWAT team, en route to assist, just two savvy unarmed policemen relying on their skills and wit to ensure a resolution. A successful outcome depended entirely on our ability to read the situation well, negotiate and to react appropriately as this progressed through each minute stage.

'Stephen,' I called out to him. 'We just want to talk.'

'Fuck off,' came the predictable response.

'We just want to get this thing sorted without anybody getting hurt,' I said, continuing our strategy of trying to establish a rapport.

These exchanges continued through the closed door for about a half hour.

'We're just going to open the door to talk properly with you,' Tom tried again.

Silence.

It was then that I slowly turned the handle and half-opened the door, leaving it ajar for protection should he advance towards us. We needed to be proactive; waiting there in the hall all evening was not an option.

Silver stood on the far side of the room, his knees slightly crouched, the samurai sword still held out in front of him, elbows locked straight. The blade extended from his joined hands at waist-height on the hilt to where his nose should have been visible to us but was obscured by his motorcycle helmet visor. He remained motionless and silent and now wore a leather motorcycle jacket. The only sign he was feeling the pressure was the fact his helmet visor was misting up. It was a warm evening and must have been almost unbearable underneath his leather jacket and crash helmet.

Suddenly, he changed position, taking two steps to his right, thus moving himself out of our line of vision. Quickly seizing the initiative again, Tom nudged the door fully open with his foot. Silver had retreated behind the sofa, his sword still in hand. Thus protected by the sofa, we moved into the room, where we presented ourselves as unarmed and unthreatening. Silver appeared to respond as he leaned back against the wall, seemingly drained from his exertions. In any confrontation it was always possible to read traces of violent intent from a person's eyes, but we were hampered by the closed visor.

'Stephen, open the visor so we can talk to you properly,' I said.

Nothing, just the sound of gasping behind the plastic and metal of the padded visored helmet.

Then, suddenly, he flicked open the visor before returning his hand to the sword hilt. He didn't speak. By this stage the encounter was now extending into its second hour.

'Listen, if you drop the sword we can get all of this sorted,' I coaxed, continuing our patient yet persistent approach, his eyes displaying a wild unpredictability.

Unexpectedly, he replied, speaking for the first time since our arrival, albeit semi-coherently, and to make a demand rather than a concession.

'Get him away from the window,' he said. 'I want nobody staring in at me.'

I gave Billy a thumbs-up, and he stood back. Our deliberate strategy was beginning to pay off.

'Okay, it's all clear now,' I said, 'it's just myself, yourself and Tom.'

'Come on,' added Tom, cajoling him a little further. 'This has gone on long enough, just put the sword down and we can all relax and have a chat.'

His arms relaxed as he let the sword drop, the samurai blade curved downwards on the couch's soft cushions. His intensity seemed to be easing even while he retained his double-handed grip on the hilt.

It was immaterial whether the gesture was intentional or not, it was a positive development. Now that the room was fully visible, I could see the walls plastered with martial arts posters of Bruce Lee's taut, sinewed and bare-chested features. In one, he held a nunchaku, a Japanese weapon with two metal sticks joined at their ends by a chain.

Silver's bright red face was drenched with sweat, droplets running down his brow to the end of his nose. His arms and shoulders lacked the charged tension from earlier, and apart from a kitchen knife, there didn't seem to be any weapons other than his. But even with the samurai sword threat receding, it was a reasonable guess that Silver had a working knowledge of martial arts, his actions suggested a propensity towards violence. It was clear that, standing at over six foot three inches in height, if aggressively disposed, his sheer physicality would prove very difficult to contain. A crash helmeted headbutt to the face would result in, at minimum, a broken nose, cracked eye socket or fractured jaw. It was still a time for extreme caution.

Still looking straight ahead, with a two-handed motion he flicked the hilt of the sword upwards and forward, and it landed on the floor close to Tom's feet with a loud metallic thud. I moved cautiously towards him, quickly pulling the sofa back out of the way to make sure there were no other weapons concealed away from view. Tom walked forward with me as I continued to talk to him. The heat was stifling in the small space, and I could feel the shirt sticking to my back.

'Okay, we are going to walk you outside with us and get some cool fresh air,' I said, placing my hand on the upper arm of his motorcycle jacket. This siege-type stand-off had reached a crucial stage and was finely balanced between violence and resolution. He looked at me warily but remained silent, his heavy breathing now relaxing into a more regular pattern. Slowly, I increased the pressure of my grip on his arm, subtly guiding him towards the door and into the hallway, on alert for any sudden movements.

The cool breeze was a welcome relief as we stepped out into the evening air, but he stopped dead as soon as we reached the gravel, appearing spooked by family members and the gardaí who had gathered.

'Tom and I are going to have a little private chat with Stephen,' I called out, motioning for them all to keep their distance. This was going well, and we didn't want it to kick off again.

'Just kneel down,' I said, guiding him over to the left. 'We'll get the helmet off you.'

He crouched down slowly, his boots scraping the gravel as he adjusted his stance. Tom held his arm as I leveraged the helmet upwards and off his head, long hair matted with sweat. The tension in his body lessened further; his posture drooped as the evening air soothed his overheated face. It was over. Perspiration fell from his nose onto his goatee beard. Billy grabbed a tea towel from the house and Silver slowly dried his forehead, face and neck.

'We're bringing you to the station and the doctor will take a look at you,' I explained, after a few minutes had passed. 'I'm going to put the cuffs on you now.'

Nodding, he placed his hands behind his neck in the pose made familiar by cinema and television.

'No, out in front is okay.'

As he watched, I clicked my handcuffs on his wrists. They made a metallic, ratcheting sound as I adjusted them to his size.

Silver was quiet on the short journey back to the station, sitting beside me in the back of the unmarked car Billy had brought over from behind the crowd. At the station, we completed the necessary paperwork before the doctor's arrival. He even calmly chatted with us and accepted the offer of a cup of tea. When, following his medical examination, the doctor committed him to the psychiatric unit at Roscommon Hospital, he went without fuss.

On our silent journey back to Castlerea station that day, we passed the Patrick Street junction where, 14 years later, Stephen Silver would yet again kneel in cinematic style. That time though, in stark, brutal contrast to the restraint and respect we had shown him, he would unleash his physical strength and violence, and pump 11 rounds of a Sig Sauer automatic handgun into the fit, healthy and vibrant body of our dear colleague and friend Garda Colm Horkan, killing him.

Unbelievably just 11 weeks after Colm's death, and just yards from where the murder took place, more Sig Sauer handguns locked and loaded filled Castlerea's Main Street with deadly menace. A white Ford Transit Connect cargo van faced in the direction of the fateful T-junction, slightly angled towards the kerb. The driver had been arrested and it lay with me to record, assess and take possession of the vehicle's deadly cargo. Pulling on latex protective gloves, I took some establishing photos of the van from both directions, thinking in advance of a jury viewing the images in a methodical sequence.

As I photographed the van from every angle I was struck by what I saw. Opening the front passenger door, a child's backpack sat in the footwell with the smiling bright eyes of Chase the PAW Patrol police dog on its front. I unzipped it fully to discover contents so far removed from childhood innocence as was imaginable. Neatly packed side by side were three fully loaded semi-automatic handguns, a Sig Sauer P224 and two Sig Sauer P226, which the driver, to wipe out a €400 drug debt, had been transporting to Dublin for a gangland hit. I retrieved the weapons and transported the deadly cache to Castlerea Garda Station as the van was towed away for further examination. Using gloved hands I placed the weapons on the conference room table, making sure to lie them on the inside surface of tamper-proof evidence bags, to avoid cross-contamination. This was the same conference table that had been the hub of the investigation in the days and weeks following Colm's murder. The camera flashgun had illuminated the stippled handgrips, the rugged raised forward-leaning striped markings on the breeches suggesting forward motion, the circular magazine release buttons indicating the payload. As I looked at the deadly arsenal before me, I contemplated the intended victim – a father, son, brother or grandson. A life no more. This was scarcely believable for the quiet rural Main Street of Castlerea, so soon following Colm's murder, three similar loaded Sig Sauer handguns present with deadly intent.

# CHAPTER 5

# TRACES OF TRUTH: TRACE EVIDENCE

On 14 October 1996, the body of Mr Richie Barron, a cattle dealer, was located on the side of the road in Raphoe, County Donegal. The scene was left unpreserved by the attending gardaí (i.e. not sealed off in advance of a technical examination by crime scene investigators) and the state pathologist was not called to examine the body. The fact that the investigation into his death was botched led to the establishment of a public tribunal of enquiry chaired by Mr Justice Frederick Morris, now commonly referred to as the Morris Tribunal. This process resulted in disquiet, disgrace and dismissals.

Ten weeks after Mr Barron's death, on 23 December, the body of Mme Sophie Toscan du Plantier was discovered at 10 a.m. in the front garden of her isolated rural cottage outside Toormore, Schull, West Cork. She had been savagely and repeatedly bludgeoned to death by somebody with the strength and power to overcome a healthy young woman in her prime who likely fought for her life. The scene, which should have yielded plenty of forensic evidence to assist in the investigation, was compromised and nothing was found to connect any suspect to the case in the subsequent murder enquiry. Furthermore, the state pathologist Dr John Harbison was unable to attend the scene until 28 hours later; when he did, he discovered 'laceration and swelling of the brain, fracture of the skull, and multiple blunt force head injuries'. This led to calls for more support for the Office of the State Pathologist.

In the intervening 28 years, rarely did a week go by without some aspect of the investigation being raised. Countless internal garda reviews, High Court libel actions, High Court extradition hearings, books, newspaper articles, news programmes and, in more recent years, podcasts added to the mountain of material surrounding the case. The Morris Tribunal laid bare the disastrous and shameful consequences following the failure to preserve and properly investigate the scene of Mr Barron's death, resulting in the decision to establish crime scene investigation units in every garda division countrywide.

American forensic pathologist Dr James Claude Upshaw Downs once said:

> You only get one chance to do it right – the first time, so you'd better do it right. In short, if you think of it, do it, or have a good reason why you didn't. Because if you don't, someone who gets paid considerably more than you and by the hour, will ask why you didn't.

Crime scene investigation begins with the identification, documentation, collection and preservation of physical evidence that links suspects to the victims and locations of crimes. Proper scene security ensures integrity and reduces the possibility that evidence may be destroyed, lost or go undetected during the investigation.

Up until 2004, only the Technical Bureau based at Garda Headquarters attended the scenes of suspicious deaths. Established in 1934, it was based at the Old Royal Hospital Infirmary building at St John's Road, Kilmainham, Dublin. These early pioneers in crime scene investigation were exceptional in many ways and had an insatiable desire to pass on their learning to others. The first officer-in-charge, Superintendent Patrick Sheridan, had studied under the renowned Swedish criminologist Dr Henry Soderman. He was followed by Superintendent George Lawlor, a respected figure in the world of scientific crime detection, who served with distinction, contributing to several scientific journals. The role was subsequently taken on by Superintendent Dan Stapleton, a legend in his own lifetime. Winning All-Ireland senior hurling championship medals in 1904, 1905 and 1907, he qualified as a chemist in 1912 and opened a business in Kilkenny. A lieutenant in the IRA during the War of Independence, he made explosives, serviced weapons and refurbished ammunition, before serving as a commandant in the Irish Free State Army. Seconded from the army, he spent 17 years in the Garda Technical Bureau gaining international recognition for his work on the 'moulage process', a system he developed for the identification of glass particles which featured in the 1940 edition of *Scientific Aids to Criminal Investigation*, published by the British Home Office.

Recent refurbishment of the old St John's Road building led to the discovery of a scale model of the La Mancha house in Malahide, County Dublin, in which six people were murdered in March 1926. This demonstrated the innovation of the investigators of the day, and how it led to Henry McCabe being identified as the murderer and sentenced to hang on 9 December 1926.

The rollout of garda crime scene investigation units countrywide only commenced in earnest in 2004. Now each garda division was to be provided with its own autonomous unit, fully resourced with the equipment and know-how to professionally process crime scenes. A programme was devised under the supervision and instruction of experts from the Garda Technical Bureau and Forensic Science Ireland, involving comprehensive training in photography, fingerprints, ballistics, fire scene investigation, blood spatter analysis and DNA sample retrieval. Further advanced courses were provided at the forensic training faculty at the University of Durham.

Our unit was one of the last to be set up and in 2007, following 17 years of frontline policing, I was given the opportunity to become a crime scene investigator. This was and is a tough job and not for the fainthearted. Not only does attendance at scenes of the most gruesome horror require strength of character and deep reserves of resilience, but the constant return visits to such harrowing sights requires repeated measured application of those qualities. The job involves painstaking attention to detail and my training courses were geared towards analysis and observation; the key exhortation was to never rush anything. The reality often involved attending to serious incidents with pressure from senior management for an early result. Yet, unless the absolute integrity of the chain of custody was watertight, from trace evidence located at scenes through to laboratory analysis and production at trial, the case would falter. That burden of responsibility lay squarely on the crime scene investigator's shoulders. Already experienced in murder scenes of the highest profile, I was now back in the midst of the most serious and critical incidents with death my constant shadow.

One of our duties as crime scene investigators involved invoking sections of the Criminal Justice (Forensic Evidence and DNA

Database System) Act 2014 to obtain a buccal swab from certain categories of prisoners detained at garda stations for interview. The process required opening a sterile swab with a foam tip and requesting the co-operation of the prisoner in question. The recent amazing advances in DNA technology were an excellent resource in the crime scene investigators armour.

In 15 years of taking such samples, I never had a prisoner refuse to comply with the buccal swab procedure. Likewise for fingerprints. A good rapport while walking from the cells worked wonders, especially when I was asking a suspect to open wide for the purposes of placing a foam-tipped swab on the inside of their cheek. Blue nitrile gloves offered little protection against a mouthful of sharp teeth. The casual uniform probably helped – black polo shirts and cargo pants automatically differentiated us from others – and the secret seemed to be to never display judgement of the crimes for which they were detained. Often they would open up about their lives, families and the paths which led to this juncture.

On 3 July 2011, Detective Garda Orla Geraghty was sitting in an unmarked detective branch car on Main Street, Longford, when she felt the force of a dark Volvo ramming into the car parked behind hers, shunting it forward and impacting her vehicle from the rear. Looking left, she saw the Volvo accelerating away at high speed and, immediately recognising the driver, circulated the details. It was 3:15 a.m.

Approximately 24 kilometres away, the residents of Ballymahon slept soundly, with only the statue of Oliver Goldsmith to watch over the main thoroughfare of his native town – leg crossed, book lowered in his right hand, a lofty gaze from his elevated plinth.

In a nearby peaceful residential estate, a hardworking truck driver, Seamus Higgins, was sleeping soundly at his home after a long day's work, his well-cared-for seven-year-old Mercedes safely parked in the driveway, when a sound half-woke him. But it was the second sound, coming from the sitting room directly below, that had him sit bolt upright. Dressing quickly, he ran downstairs to investigate and, looking into the sitting room, he saw that his new flat screen TV had been removed from its wall fitting. On into the kitchen at the rear of the house, where his eyes were drawn to the open sliding patio door from where the intruder had entered.

'Imagination, of course, can open any door – turn the key and let terror walk right in,' wrote Truman Capote. Sometimes this can happen in reality too. Suddenly, a hooded figure emerged from the shadows and, and in what seemed like a single sweeping move, a gloved hand forcefully restrained Seamus as the glint of a large blade pressed against his throat. This was the stuff of nightmares, an armed intruder in the dead of the night, the sanctuary of the home violated with physical confrontation.

A smell of alcohol from the raider's breath accompanied words delivered with a strong Dublin accent in a menacing tone and magnified by the silent surroundings in the still of night: 'Get back up those stairs or I'll fucking kill you.' Ten seconds of stand-off ensued as both gauged the other's likely reaction, an abrupt shove backwards breaking the impasse. Quickly retreating and looking out from the upstairs window, Seamus watched as his Mercedes engine roared to life and accelerated down the road, the last time it would ever leave his driveway. The lights of a dark Volvo immediately came on, one headlight pointing askew and the damage from the earlier incident visible, and it joined the Mercedes in a speeding convoy towards Ballymahon.

A few hours later, I pulled up outside Seamus's house, the neighbours still oblivious to the frightening drama which had played out in their slumbering midst on this quiet Sunday morning. Garda Anthony Scanlon had preserved the scene and briefed me on the fate of the stolen Mercedes, which had just been located burned out in a rural location close to Strokestown, County Roscommon. A quick glance indicated that the initial point of entry had been through a neighbour's back garden, the adjoining panel fence having been raised. Scanning the footpath and garden, a TV remote control sat on the garden verge. The telltale sign of the forced patio door lock pinpointed the entry method itself.

At that time, uPVC doors were compromised by a flawed design of the lock barrel, the centrepiece bridging both sides being but a flimsy few millimetres of thin metal. A firm twist with a vice-grips and the centre would snap and give easy access to a home. I located the damaged lock at the rear of the garden, along with the telltale vice-grip indentations on either side of it.

Carefully sliding the patio door open, nothing seemed to be too out of place as I entered. One of the large knives was missing from its place in the block, having been used earlier against its owner but, despite the seriousness of the incident, there was little enough to focus on inside the home. The television had been lifted clean from the bracket, likewise a laptop from the kitchen table. I was aware, however, that the raider had been wearing gloves, which from an investigation point of view left me in a difficult position. The forlorn hope of the detailed fingerprint examination that followed was that maybe the culprit had removed a glove during the raid. Not only that; the pressure was firmly mounting on me as I eliminated each area of interest.

Having photographed the exterior and interior of the home, I moved along. Because so little had been disturbed within the house itself, the patio door became my main area of focus. Retrieving my examination kit from the van, I knelt at it, lifting the usual mish-mash of fingerprint layers, the ordinary comings and goings of everyday life, before mounting them on fingerprint lift cards. As I shone my torch on the area around the door handle, I angled the light beam along the pane of window glass, moving it along in vertical lines, a slow painstaking advance, tracing a miniature search grid. Though the light was very bright, this was an effective technique for highlighting marks, and something caught my eye. As soon as I saw it, it was gone. But by retracing the path of the light, I spied it again – a tiny speck on the glass, about 30cm from the handle. To the naked eye it didn't look much, a spot of dirt maybe, and I reined in the hope I felt rising inside as I picked up the magnifying glass and hovered it over the tiny speck on the glass surface. There it was, in the lens of the glass: the unmistakable hue of a blood contact mark. Under magnification, it revealed a concentration of blood towards the bottom, gravity acting on this minuscule amount, the glorious dark red shade lifting my spirits.

After preparing a number of swabs, making sure to press each swab tip against the stain, I set about the painstaking process of recording and noting my progress. Then, securing them safely in their protective plastic tubing, I packaged and labelled the swabs, placing them in tamper-proof evidence bags. Samples safely secured, I set about measuring the precise location of the stain and sketching the results in my notebook.

As I was packing up to leave, Seamus Higgins returned with his partner and I sympathised with them on their ordeal. They were interested to learn about my sample, and I asked if any family member had cut themselves in the past 24 hours. No, they replied. My hopes rose even further.

Chain of custody was observed and the sample arrived securely for analysis at Forensic Science Ireland.

On 22 November 2011, I stood in front of the main suspect, Eamon Murphy, a 48-year-old Dublin native. Nothing shouted caution about the smart–casual, business-like appearance of the well-built man standing before me, neatly dressed in a smart pullover and dark jeans. We spoke about his native place in Dublin Garda K District (of television documentary renown) and how that, by the time of my posting there in 1990, his own native Cabra had quietened down and Blanchardstown was revving up.

Fingerprinting involves very close personal proximity, taking a grip of each digit and rolling them onto the inked pad to record the loops, whorls and ridges singularly unique to each person. It can't be done without the person's co-operation. With Murphy, the conversation was amiable as I inked his fingers – two fellas in their forties shooting the breeze. Intelligent, personable and perceptive, his body language was neutral and in full coordination with mine. He continued to cooperate as I took a swab and rubbed it on the inside of his mouth to gather the invisible traces that would generate a sample. As we parted, I sealed this buccal swab into an evidence bag and recorded my compliance with the legislation in my notebook. The foam-tipped swab, now adorned with epithelial cells from the inside of the suspect's cheek, would shortly be opened by a scientist at Forensic Science Ireland, where a DNA profile would be extracted.

After a painstaking investigation by the detective branch at Longford, CCTV footage at the nightclub in the town showed two men leaving the nightclub and getting into a black Volvo, which was subsequently traced to an address at Roosky, County Roscommon. The gardaí seized the car and our examination established the presence of impact damage to the front grille and displacement of the front bumper consistent with the description of the damaged front of the vehicle which Seamus Higgins saw leaving outside his house in convoy with his stolen Mercedes. A report from Forensic Science Ireland later positively identified a DNA profile from the swab of blood at the scene and after a file was submitted to the DPP, the accused was charged with the crimes.

Eamon Murphy was convicted by a jury at Longford Circuit Criminal Court on 19 February 2015 of one count of aggravated burglary and one count of unauthorised taking of a motor vehicle. On 23 October 2015, Eamon Murphy was sentenced to 10 years' imprisonment, with the final three years of that sentence suspended on conditions concerning his conviction for aggravated burglary and a one-year sentence of imprisonment concerning the unlawful taking of the vehicle. The sentences were ordered to be served concurrently. This was not the last of proceedings, however. Solicitors for Mr Murphy submitted to the Court of Criminal Appeal that the trial judge had erred in allowing evidence regarding the sample to go before the jury. They contended that the DNA swab sample was retained by An Garda Síochána in excess of the allowable statutory 12-month period, after which it should have been destroyed. However, the Court of Criminal Appeal held that the trial judge had been correct; the taking of the DNA buccal sample was compliant with all statutory laws.

———◆———

The crime scene investigation units were originally set up to process serious incidents. However, as the years passed, management in An Garda Síochána became more and more fearful that there might be something sinister behind all the sudden deaths throughout the country. We suddenly found our role expanding to encompass almost every type of fatality, including suicides, to ensure no foul play could be alleged. The call would come in: 'Listen, we have a sudden death here and the superintendent wants you to take a look.' My first question would always be, 'Is it suspicious?' to which the reply would generally be, ' Ah no, not really, it's just the Super would be happier if you took a look.'

Cases involving non-fatal crimes, such as rape, sexual assault, aggravated burglary, robbery, serious assault, criminal damage and arson, were a staple of our crime scene investigations. On top of this, we gradually found ourselves being tasked with more and more death scenes, until we were attending every type of fatality imaginable, including any classification of death where the circumstances were unusual in any small way.

Over a period of 15 years, I photographed death, documented death, recorded death, viewed death and thought about death.

My fear of it was long gone but, by virtue of my job description, I was cast back to a place I had occupied before as a youth, one of contemplation, consideration and speculation on the ultimate mystery death held.

# CHAPTER 6

# SUSPICIOUS MINDS

The EU Structural Development Fund facilitated improvements to Ireland's road network at the turn of the century. In doing so, it unwittingly provided increased mobility to Dublin criminals travelling throughout the country in high-powered vehicles. There was widespread shock and revulsion at the number of vicious attacks on the elderly in rural communities during the 1990s and 2000s. Rural communities were gripped by fear and trepidation as the most vulnerable were seemingly picked off in sequence in cowardly robberies and attacks. A compounding factor to this trend was the fact that some elderly people hoarded significant sums of cash at home, which they had set aside incrementally over the years. Not alone were their homes being broken into and their personal contents plundered; elderly occupants were often tied up and brutalised as the burglars attempted to establish the location of their savings. These cowardly robberies frequently went wrong and resulted in tragic deaths.

I doubted these criminals deliberately set out to commit murder, but youthful strength and adrenaline, combined with alcohol and drugs during the course of robberies, along with the frailty, vulnerability and weakness of their elderly victims, often resulted in outcomes such as the savage killing of Mr Paddy Logan at Castlejordan, County Meath on 5 June 2000 for the princely sum of £45. On 20 July 2002, the *Irish Times* reported on the sentencing hearing of the perpetrators, both of whom had form for this type of crime:

Two brothers who robbed elderly people were jailed for a total of 27 years yesterday for the killing of an 81-year-old farmer who was beaten to death for £45. Sentencing John Doyle to 15 years and his brother, Christopher Doyle, to 12 years for the manslaughter of Co. Meath farmer Mr Paddy Logan on June 5th, 2000, Mr Justice Carney said no sentence he could impose would adequately deal with the horror of this case. The two were further sentenced to three years for the robbery of Mr Logan's 85-year-old brother, Peter, who was injured in the attack. The court heard that John Doyle was previously convicted of stabbing to death an 84-year-old man in Dublin in 1984. He was also convicted of the burglary of an elderly couple in England, an offence which happened after the killing of Mr Logan.

Christopher Doyle also has lengthy convictions for violent crimes, including that of beating an elderly woman after he broke into the bedroom of her home in England. The court heard the defendants are from a family of settled Travellers whose mother sent John out to steal when he was seven years old …

At the Central Criminal Court yesterday, Mr Peter Logan had to be helped to the stand to give evidence of how his life was destroyed by the killing of his brother. The court heard he sustained a fractured nose in the attack and since then is on anti-depressants. He also suffers from recurring flashbacks and nightmares … Mr Justice Carney said: 'For the sake of

£45 the life of one man was snuffed out and his brother had his destroyed.' The Doyles then engaged in the 'cut-throat defence' of blaming each other.

The accompanying photograph of Christopher Doyle triggered a memory of the man when he was younger. The first time I arrested him was around 1992 and he was approximately 14 years old. Curiosity tweaked, I retrieved the old evidence bag and was transported back to those days by the sight of the small hand-held notebook, its pages now yellowed with time and my handwriting shaky as I adjusted to writing notes in it.

The entry was dated 12 June 1992. I was in the passenger seat of a patrol car with Garda Mick Clancy, a seasoned Kerryman of 30 years' service, when we observed the youthful, tanned features of Christopher Doyle pedalling furiously on a bicycle he had just forcibly taken from its owner a short distance away. The call with the description had come across the garda radio and Mick expertly wheeled the patrol car around, the oncoming traffic yielding, and gained quickly on the youthful fugitive, his pedal power no match for the powerful engine. Our advantage was short-lived as dust and gravel forced us to slow down as we entered St Francis's Park on the slip road adjacent to Nutgrove Shopping Centre, home to about ten Traveller families. Immediately Christopher dropped the bike, half skidding, half falling, and took off running as he regained his balance, his stumble allowing me to pursue him on foot. I gained on him as he headed towards the open door of his family caravan, two scrawny dogs joining in the pursuit and the quickly gathering onlookers now roaring for Christopher.

I jumped through the open door of the caravan, just missing his trailing leg, and was greeted by an almighty cursing roar from his mother who, for a large, heavy-set woman, was speedy in thought and action. The dinner plate in her hand was quickly and expertly flung through the air and smashed off my back as I exited the far window after Christopher. We landed in a tangle of plastic flower arrangements, net curtains, dirt and dust, the wind temporarily knocked from our lungs.

Roars followed from his mother, her protective instincts now fully activated, as I bundled Christopher into the patrol car's back seat. Mick, knowing how these matters generally played out, had the recovered bike loaded in the boot, with the patrol car faced for off. We quickly departed with an escort of baying dogs at each wing and the thumps of assorted missiles hitting the patrol car as we exited. The accompanying roars of the onlookers joined in a triumphant cheer as a Coca Cola can struck the windscreen, its fizzed contents spraying as we departed.

Christopher was calm after his exertions and when we later processed him at the garda station, I had little inkling that he would grow in adulthood to become a violent killer. Christopher's strength was evident then though. While not tall, his already muscular frame would have provided ample resistance had he chosen that route. Yet he was pleasant and well-mannered, betraying no hint of aggression or hostility, just a subdued demeanour that befitted someone who'd been caught with the stolen bicycle and would have to face his mother later. I can still recall his father coming to collect him later at the station. Bill Doyle was a Dubliner who married into the Traveller tradition. Greying hair quiffed in a rockabilly style, he had a calm manner and there was a strangeness to his gaze on account of one of his pupils being permanently dilated – the legacy of an accident. His black leather jacket added some bulk to his slight, wiry frame as he promised that there would be no more trouble from Christopher.

It was against this backdrop of outrage and horror at these attacks on the rural elderly that I attended one of my first crime scenes as a member of the Divisional Crime Scene Investigation Unit in 2007. Detective Inspector Pat Finlay's name flashed up on the screen of the old Nokia phone as I was preparing to finish my shift – it was often the case that serious incidents were reported towards the end of one. A methodical and detailed investigator with his own unique way of parsing and analysing policing matters, I had first met him in my early days at Blanchardstown Garda Station, Dublin Metropolitan 'K' District. By 2007, he had responsibility for all serious crime in the then Roscommon/Galway East garda policing division and was one of the first senior investigating officers (SIO) to be appointed countrywide. He was the first point of contact when there was any suggestion of a suspicious death or foul play in that area.

Pat outlined to me the situation. Local gardaí had attended the scene at a remote rural cottage, where the body of an elderly male had been discovered in what appeared to be questionable circumstances. Pat went on to explain that conditions were poor at the scene and that he had no further information for me other than that the attending gardaí were concerned that violence may have been inflicted on the man prior to his death.

In such instances, responsibility for making the call as to whether the circumstances of the death were problematic or otherwise lay with the crime scene investigator. We would normally work in pairs but, because of the lateness of the call, I was on my own. This was potentially a very serious scene and I was acutely aware that the decision as to whether the services of the Office of the State Pathologist were needed would be mine alone. There was a palpable reluctance on the part of some local garda management at that time to engage the state pathologist in case it turned out that the situation was not suspicious after all. During my tenure as a crime scene investigator, my colleagues and I quickly dispensed with such thinking and would request the state pathologist to attend even if we had only the slightest doubt in our minds regarding the circumstances of death. As time passed and our experience in dealing with these incidents increased, our confidence in making these calls grew, in no small part due to the excellent working relationship that we had built up with the state pathologist herself, Dr Marie Cassidy, and her deputy Dr Mike Curtis. Both Marie and Mike always expressed a preference for being called early to any prospective suspicious death scene, so as to avoid non-forensic hospital pathologists commencing a post-mortem, and then concluding that the death might indeed have been dubious. Yet this was always tempered with an awareness of their workload and our determination not to erode their goodwill by requesting unnecessary callouts.

Although I had just recently completed my crime scene investigation training, I was confident in my ability to process the scene and make an assessment as to whether the death was suspicious. I was also well aware of the climate at the time where attacks on the vulnerable elderly were widespread; I knew that my deliberations would be eagerly anticipated. The fact I had been present at so many death scenes during my early years as a frontline garda lent an assurance and experience to my initial forays in my new role. In this regard the gardaí had a distinct advantage over other police forces that employed civilian-trained scientists as crime scene investigators. Our experience as frontline officers before crime scene investigation gave us a deep feel for the subtleties of crime scenes. I had been first at the scene of several murders while stationed in the Dublin Metropolitan Region and in this work had been exposed to the attention to detail required, both at the initial investigation stage and any subsequent murder trial hearing. I was well prepared for my new role. In later years, when garda management was considering civilianising all 154 crime scene investigators in Ireland, I made this argument forcefully in a document circulated to senior management and the notion was subsequently shelved.

I loaded my equipment into the van, double-checking each item to ensure I wasn't left short in an isolated rural area. It was all necessary: the white personal protective overalls, gloves, Nikon D 200 digital camera and spare battery pack, waterproof gear, wellingtons, and my personal issue crime scene investigation kit box containing the all-important A4 hardback notebook, fingerprint powders and lift cards, as well as assorted swabs and containers for DNA retrieval purposes. Most significantly this late at night, I unplugged our heavy-duty halogen crime scene lamp from its charging station, distinctive with its weight and bright yellow colour with blue trim. Then, locking the office door, I began the hour-long drive that would take me to the scene. Crime scene investigators possess a clear advantage in our capacity to process an upsetting or difficult scene: usually, we're not the ones to discover the body, or even the first personnel at the scene. As well as this, the silent journey to the scene allowed for the processing of thoughts; briefings received helped prepare the mind for any eventuality. This advantage was often eroded by the amount of time we would spend alone with the deceased, however, often in sub-optimal circumstances, especially in cases where the passing was tragic, violent or self-inflicted.

En route, I received a call from the local sergeant who was preserving the scene, who gave me directions to the remote rural location. These were the days before Eircodes or GPS navigation systems and we had to be expert at decoding the vaguest of directions.

As I turned the van into the isolated driveway, I was immediately struck by the complete darkness of this typical farm cottage. All I could see was the reflection of fluorescent jackets in the headlights – local gardaí preserving the scene and preventing unauthorised access as the crime scene tape swayed in the light breeze. As I approached the cottage the sergeant confirmed that there was no electricity. My immediate impression was that this was more likely due to the neglect of the resident rather than any sinister attempt by a prospective assailant. While it wasn't unusual for power and phone lines to be disconnected in break-ins to business premises, it seemed unlikely in this case.

Exiting the van and putting on my white protective suit and gloves, I confirmed with the gardaí present some details of the case I'd already been given – marks on the body and how the scene inside was difficult to assess. I was also told that the body had been discovered by a neighbour who regularly called to check in on the deceased.

Initial impressions were already forming, a process that was grounded in my many years' experience of other crime scenes, as well as an instinct for anything which might appear out of the ordinary or simply odd and strange. It was the rough equivalent of a computer programme running through a database of previous information, but in the case of the crime scene investigator it was about a lived and worked gut feeling that came from years of exposure to death scenes. This internal radar was developed and honed to such an extent that even though a scene might initially appear normal, a feeling akin to a sixth sense could present for any little thing which seemed 'off'. It was always important to permit the facts of a crime scene to speak for themselves – to avoid theories, notions or suggestions at that point, all of which could cloud your perception of what was actually there.

A quick visual inspection of the house exterior, aided by the bright halogen search lamp, revealed no evidence of a break-in or forced entry. The sergeant explained that the deceased had not been seen for a number of days and that the front door of the cottage was open on arrival. As I stood by the entranceway, I was conscious of the gaze on me from those present – the local gardaí and neighbours who had gathered.

A good crime scene investigator should be able to discern what is hidden and observe what has been displaced. However, sometimes specific circumstances of a case can complicate these important duties. This was one such case. The layout of the living room was in the traditional old Irish cottage format, a large open fireplace to the right, the kitchen table inside the front door under the window, and a couch towards the centre of the room, side-on to the fireplace. This was close to the only normal aspect of the scene before me. Before becoming a policeman, I had little idea that people could live in such poor conditions. It was not unusual to come upon dreadful living conditions, especially among elderly bachelors residing alone, an unfortunate symptom of extreme isolation and loneliness, with the poor conditions often going unnoticed by the person concerned.

To describe the conditions of that isolated cottage living room, in which I stood, sketching and taking notes, as poor would be an understatement. A quick look in the adjoining rooms confirmed that it was also the kitchen, living room and bedroom all combined. The entire floor was covered with boxes, bed clothing, rubbish bags, clothing, empty milk cartons, cereal boxes, shopping bags and every type of household waste imaginable, alongside assorted bags of turf, coal and firewood. The difficulty with this scene was not in discerning whether anything was out of place, here everything was out of place. The smell of a turf fire lingered in the air and the walls were darkened with many years of grime and dust.

On the far side of the sofa, barely visible from the doorway due to the volume of waste, lay the body of the deceased, fully clothed. He was a man in his late seventies or early eighties and, although he had not been seen in the recent past, there was no evidence of decomposition having commenced. This did not necessarily mean that he had died recently; the cold temperatures both inside and outside the house could have slowed the rate of decay. Picking my steps towards the body, I was careful to not disturb anything. I was also aware that there could be a murder weapon hidden from view. For a moment, I stood there in silence, the squalor of my surroundings illuminated by the powerful light of the daylight halogen crime scene lamp as its beam swept across the room. Plausible-sounding scenarios were surging forward in my mind; conscious of the dangers of making assumptions or jumping to conclusions, I pushed them away. Eventually, having soaked in the surroundings, I placed the lamp on the floor and extended the square illumination panel to its maximum height of three feet before angling its beam down on the body.

Fully clothed, surrounded by a sea of waste, it waited patiently for my evaluation.

Immediately I saw what had concerned the attending gardaí: a deep wound on the lower side of the man's left cheek and several smaller marks around his face. I loosened his clothing, concentrating initially on the head, neck and torso as I checked for signs of further injury. His lifeless open eyes staring back at me contained no sign of petechial haemorrhaging – tiny pinpoint red marks – to indicate terminal asphyxiation, a result of blood pressure that builds up inside the brain before being forced out through the eyeballs and inside of the eyelids when the airway is forcibly constricted. As I adjusted the light to eliminate some shadow that was protruding across part of his eyes, I crouched down for a closer look at the face wound. That was when something grabbed my attention. But I continued to make notes of my findings, adding a rough sketch map of the scene and body position and referencing the details of the wound. As was customary, I offered a silent reflection and prayer and hoped that the man was at peace.

Despite the chaotic nature of the scene, I was satisfied that there was no evidence of a violent struggle having taken place, though I wanted to confirm my suspicions about the deep wound on the face. I moved a few of the large boxes to allow for a clear view of the body from the doorway and collected my camera and flash gun from the van, pausing at one point to reflect on how strange it was that, given my childhood fear of death, I felt comfortable in such surroundings, confident in what I was doing, and not at all out of place. Then I double-checked my compact flash card and camera equipment before photographing the exterior of the house, which I did slowly, wanting more time to elapse before I returned inside.

Once I had approached the front door again, I adjusted the camera settings to record the interior, relying on the advanced auto-focus system to capture what I required. Edging forward silently, I paused to maintain my grip on the camera as I slowly raised it to chest height, angling it so that when the shutter was released it would capture the upper part of the body where it lay. I stood there in silence, steadying myself and listening intently. Nothing was audible but the sound of my heartbeat. Then, suddenly, in response to the sound of the motorised shutter and rapid-fire light pulses from the flash gun, there was a burst of activity and movement, and the viewing screen images confirmed my initial instincts about the cause of death and the face wounds.

After photographing the rest of the interior, the position and location of the body and the facial wound, I was satisfied that this case would not require the services of the state pathologist and that in this case we did not have a murder on our hands. Notwithstanding the large wound on the deceased's cheek, nothing suspicious or untoward had happened to this poor man and he could now be laid to rest in peace. An ordinary hospital post-mortem would most likely reveal a death by natural causes. I dialled up the old Nokia and briefed Detective Inspector Finlay, stating that it was now up to the coroner to give permission to remove the deceased for an ordinary post-mortem examination. Driving back to the office, I was satisfied that this had not been a violent or suspicious death and that, at least for now, the rural elderly community to which the deceased belonged could rest easy. I wrote up my records content with the outcome of my first solo outing as a fully fledged crime scene investigator and looked forward to my day off and a good sleep in anticipation of a hard day's work in the garden.

Often when things went wrong for gardaí or pressure was applied from external sources, management's apprehension was palpable. The next morning, the hospital pathologist had contacted the local superintendent's office and expressed concerns about the body from the rural isolated cottage which had been presented for post-mortem earlier that morning, stating that there were suspicions about wounds and marks on the body. I was directed to be in University College Hospital Galway at 2:00 p.m. for a consultation with the pathologist. The garden would have to wait. Driving to the hospital, I replayed the previous night's scene, again reaching the conclusion that there was nothing suspicious about the death. The pathologist declined my outstretched hand of introduction with a nod towards his own gloved hands which appeared clear of any contamination. Dispensing with niceties, he outlined his suspicions about the facial wounds and suggested it be preferable for the state pathologist to carry out a forensic post-mortem. While certainly aware of their willingness to attend scenes and post-mortems on request, I did not feel comfortable securing their services in circumstances where the hospital pathologist was perfectly capable of carrying out the examination. This was clearly one such case and I respectfully and firmly stood my ground. Keen to show just who was knowledgeable in these matters, he proceeded to describe how the wounds clearly represented suspicious activity prior to death. I held firm, stating that if the wound had been caused by a violent assault, why had there been an absence of any blood at the scene or on the body?

Sensing a momentary hesitation, I placed on the table photographs taken from the cottage doorway and watched as the pathologist recoiled. The first image showing a rodent perched on the deceased's cheek and feeding on the wound. Two others on his chest had likewise been disturbed by the camera shutter and flashgun. The next, a close-up of the deceased's eyes revealed a rodent dropping, slightly obscured by the pupil but clearly visible in the illuminated flashlight. Based on this evidence, it was clear that in the time between the man's death and the discovery of his body the rodents had started to bite him, resulting in the suspicious-looking wounds on his face.

My offer to leave the images was quickly declined and the post-mortem was carried out promptly with a result of 'death by natural causes' declared. If nothing else, this episode confirmed that my instincts for the crime scene investigator role were sound and that my long years of frontline policing experience in Dublin, with its fair share of death, trauma and tragedy, would stand me in good stead. The all-important sixth sense or gut feeling which came from such exposure was alive and functioning well inside me.

Remarkably, my last death scene before I retired resulted in a similar outcome, with a pathologist again shirking responsibility and attempting to foist another unsuspicious death onto the state pathologist. In that sad case, a man had died alone. His right arm and leg were deep into the decomposition process, while his skin appearing alive, as it housed a writhing, squirming colony of maggots and larvae. I suspect the hospital pathologist had no stomach for closer inspection.

I often reflected on the young Christopher Doyle starting out in life, strong, handsome and tanned of complexion, pleasant in his general demeanour and wondered how his life spiralled. The *Irish Times* article stated that he was a father of many children and I hoped that the same cycle would not be repeated for them. I thought of his innocent elderly victims, alone and afraid as brothers inflicted cruelty on other brothers and hoped that the scourge of this crime would be eradicated from our midst. I contemplated the lonely existence and isolation of so many vulnerable elderly throughout our country and how it led to the conditions which prevailed in that cottage. I realised too that this issue wasn't confined to rural areas, and that sometimes it could be hidden in plain view. Some day we too could be that frail person and wouldn't it be nice to think that no matter what we would never be abandoned in such conditions?

Although certain I could trust my own professional judgement under pressure, other issues swirled around the back of my mind. Could exposure to future horrific scenes of death, trauma and tragedy trigger some variation of post-traumatic stress disorder? Could my childhood fear of death reappear? Or would my ability to stay calm, rationalise, compartmentalise and efficiently deal with things keep such issues firmly at bay? I was about to find out.

# CHAPTER 7

# NATIONAL TREASURES

t was 27 March 2009. The wide streets were deserted as the van edged slowly towards some parked cars, the driver cutting the engine as everything returned to silence. Both he and its single passenger sat cautiously for a few minutes, shadowy figures just out of the streetlamp beam, an earlier drive-by having revealed no threat. They moved silently and purposefully along the path with dark clothing and snugly fitted balaclavas, their headtorches primed and a trusty jemmy bar, heavy bolt cutters and flathead screwdriver in their hands. The pharmacy would be an easy touch.

Only a small metal gate and old-style wooden front door stood in their way. Adrenaline flowing and hearts thumping, one last scan of the street and they were ready. A quick snip of the bolt cutters and the lock fell away, the metal gate opening smoothly without a noise. With a swift wrenching movement of the jemmy bar, the door lock ceded, the silence broken by pieces of wood splintering and falling to the ground. A firm boot to the centre of the double doors and they were in.

Straining for a moment, to catch any internal alarm activation that might have gone off, all they could hear was their thumping hearts. One kept watch by the door as the other scooped the till's meagre contents into the canvas holdall, coins spilling and rolling across the floor, a quick search of usual hiding places failing to yield any further bonus. The far shelves were lined with branded perfumes, toiletries and aftershaves, Armani, Lacoste, Dior,

Tommy Hilfiger, all of which would appeal to black market street sellers. These too got swept into the holdall.

The lookout threw him another bag as he proceeded to the dispensary, prescription drugs being of greater value on the streets. He loaded up with paracetamol, codeine, cough syrups and other medications. As his headtorch beam swept the room it landed on a metal object in the corner: a safe. It was old, heavy and well-made, and a hefty tug confirmed it was locked and weighty. He ran through the door with the canvas holdalls, his lookout hot on his heels, and as they fired the bags into the van they grabbed their trolley. The coast was still clear as they returned to the dispensary, where it took both of them to tilt the safe just enough for the trolley to slide underneath, the tipping point on the fulcrum rendering it practically weightless. Making it to the van they pivoted the safe onto the rear sill until balanced and then slid it fully in.

The driver eased the van smoothly onto the road and worked gently through the gears as they made their getaway towards Dublin. They were clear now, easy did it and all would be well. The fleeing raiders had little inkling that they would soon be connected to mysterious events from another era entirely.

The nearby raised peat bogland at Coggalbeg was just a few kilometres from Cruachan Aí, Rathcroghan, renowned for its collection of more than 240 archaeological sites ranging across a time span of 5,500 years. Not only was it a significant gathering place for Ireland's high kings, queens, chieftains and their warrior tribes over the millennia, Cruachan Aí, Rathcroghan was a mystical and sacred burial site, containing 37 identified bronze and iron age burial mounds, as well as a place of medieval significance, with sites including Tulsk Dominican Priory.

If you place a ruler on a map between Cruachan Aí, Rathcroghan, and the Hill of Uisneach, Loughnavalley, County Westmeath, the line will cross Coggalbeg raised bogland. Peat deposits formed there around 10,000 years ago and it borders an area of extraordinarily fertile land known historically as the plains of Connacht.

Set upon a layer of calcium-rich limestone bedrock and providing vital mineral supplements for quicker bone development, the soil here provided rich grass on which livestock thrived. No wonder it has been an area of continued human habitation over 6,000 years through the neolithic, bronze and iron ages to today. While situated along the boundary that marked the division in the Middle Ages between two of the O'Connor clan branches, a burial stone outside Tulsk dating at 5,000 years old clearly demonstrates that this area had been an ancient sacred site even before that. The adjoining boglands were considered mystical and fearful spaces where a connecting gateway to the spirit world was thought to exist. Indeed, it was said that the very festival of Samhain (Halloween) originated there at Uaimh na gCat.

Fourteen years after the raid of the pharmacy, I went to visit the bogland at Coggalbeg. It was early June 2023 and a beautiful spell of warm weather had settled over Ireland. A narrow overgrown pathway to the raised peat bog made a swift transition from finest grass farmland to a terrain so soft it gave a pleasant spring underfoot. I sat on a low bank of peat topped with heather in yellow and purple hues, which had replaced the subdued tones of winter, and scribbled some notes mapping the passage of time since these peatlands first formed. I couldn't make much headway because I was considering a period of prehistory for which there was no documented record to reference, the earliest written historical accounts having only arrived with Christianity after AD 400. The investigator in me tried to eliminate the unlikely and focus on the evidence, but again I drew a blank. There was silence except for the buzz of a colourful dragonfly which suddenly stopped and hovered in front of me before departing, his droning fading into the distance. I closed my eyes, the warm sun on my face, and imagined an event which had actually happened there thousands of years before, at the very location where I sat.

A shadowy figure was hard at work following the orders of his chieftain who watched on. Their covert task was to deposit in this place of transition certain precious items as an offering of gratitude in accordance with custom. It was sunrise, a safer time than darkness to enter such places, and he carefully placed the cloth covering on the ground before slicing his tool into the soft peat bogland, removing a number of block-like rectangles and placing them to the side. He carefully opened the cloth, light reflecting on the beautiful crescent-shaped piece with delicate etchings carved on its thin surface. Two smaller items were circular – disc-shaped gold – with a raised cross motif. He stepped back respectfully as the chieftain, a man of status and power who had provided well for his people, chanted the accompanying prayer, placed his offering in the depository and signalled for the block-like rectangles of peat to be replaced. They turned and walked away, their task completed.

In the summer of 1945, Hubert Lannon was halfway through a hard day's work cutting turf on his plot at Coggalbeg. Slowly and methodically, he sliced his slane through the soft peat, and laid his cuts out in neat rows to dry as turf. His eye was caught by something golden embedded in the peat bank. He carefully cleared around it with his hands, wiping its delicate surface clean, exposing it to the daylight for the first time in 4,000 years before placing it gently on the ground beside him.

The outline of two more objects were revealed which he also retrieved. Where did they come from and how long had they been there? Hubert stood for a while admiring their craftmanship before placing them safely to one side and continuing with his work. Another few hours wait wouldn't do them any harm, the turf needed saving for the winter ahead.

The morning of 27 March 2009 was shaping up to be a busy one. While there were no fatalities or serious physical harm incidents waiting for crime scene investigation, I had received other requests for our services and started by prioritising those business premises that had been broken into overnight. Sheehan's in Strokestown, County Roscommon, was first on my list. As I pulled up across the street I was struck by the building's well-preserved exterior and traditional facade. The name sign was painted bright red in contrast with the white walls and black quoin stones and trim. The raised wooden letters of 'SHEEHAN'S CHEMIST' appeared very old and had been fitted to look as if they were floating rather than attached to the backboard.

Entering the shop was like stepping back into a time capsule and I took a few moments to savour the atmosphere. A decorative terrazzo floor lay between the most beautiful sets of display cabinets, evoking childhood memories of places with a similar traditional style. Set at waist level, dark wooden frames held the glass counter-level display and complementary dark wooden shelving cabinets surrounded the premises. Each cabinet and shelving drawer had traditional circular brass fittings with circular recessed handles, which required just the gentlest grasp and twist to release the mechanism. Over the years, I had seen premises trashed in the frenzied rush to steal and get out, but in this case the raiders had blessedly not damaged any of the precious fittings.

Someone was speaking on the phone in the rear office, and I patiently waited for the conversation to end. Sunniva Sheehan soon came to attend me and I was immediately struck by her striking elegance and presence. I expressed my sympathies about the break-in and explained that I was a crime scene investigator seeking forensic evidence to help with the enquiry. She detailed the large quantity of perfumes and aftershaves stolen along with both prescription and non-prescription medication. She was relieved, however, that there had been little cash on the premises as she had deposited the week's takings in the bank only the previous afternoon. Then she pointed out where her safe had been taken from, noting that it only contained documentation.

Conscious that she had a business to run, I assured Sunniva that I would conduct my examination as quickly as possible. Then I complimented her on the premise's stunning interiors.

'As well as a pharmacist, my father was a skilled craftsman

and built them in the 1920s. He also hand carved the name sign lettering over the front door.'

When I indicated amazement at both the talent required and that it had survived to this day, she chuckled.

'Ah, many's the time sales reps tried to get me to pull out the cabinets, but that will never happen.'

After collecting my equipment from the van, I began my examination of the metal half-gate attached to the outer entrance frame. I secured the lock, which had been removed with a bolt cutter, the telltale sign visible on the curved metallic locking mechanism, and placed it in an evidence bag, which I labelled. Then, turning to the gate's surface, I spread a layer of powder on the surface, revealing some fingermarks. By virtue of its location it had been handled many times and the fingermarks had blended together.

Removing some white fingerprint lift cards, I opened a fresh roll of clear lifting tape, stronger than the ordinary commercial product and designed to unfurl very smoothly and avoid striations on the tape surface. I placed the sticky side down across the surface of the powdered area, smoothed it into place and then delicately lifted and placed it onto the white lift card.

I repeated this process at the front metal gate and the front double doors at the point of access. I also took paint samples from the splintered wood and documented them. The possibility of a defence's senior counsel later sharpening their verbal claws at my expense had me carefully dating and describing the location of each fingermark on the rear of the lift cards and making a corresponding record in my notebook.

Sunniva approached as I moved my equipment inside.

'I was onto a sister of mine and as we were chatting we remembered that there is something valuable missing with the safe.' She described a gold crescent-shaped artefact and two gold discs, which had been found by a local man while cutting turf and handed in to her father in 1947.

As I continued dusting for fingerprints indoors, my mind returned to national school and the drawing in my fourth-class copy book of an object similar to that described by Sunniva. I racked my brain for the name but it wouldn't come. It was tantalisingly just out of reach, rusty neurons and synapses sparking life into a segment of my memory long since filed.

Whether or not the contents of a package dropped by the raiders as they filled their holdall helped, suddenly the name came to me. It was a gold lunula and, combined with the gold discs, I realised they were priceless artefacts. I was conscious of the pre-historical significance of nearby Rathcroghan and the many discoveries of precious artefacts in the boglands of this region. And I knew it was a lunula based on the description, having seen them in the National Museum. I phoned Detective Inspector Pat Finlay in Roscommon Garda Station.

'I'm here at Sheehan's and I think there's something very valuable missing with the safe.' I paused for dramatic effect.

'Yeah, go on', he said.

'It's worth more than the total combined value of every pharmacy raid in Ireland, ever', I continued, enjoying the mental tease.

'What are you on about?' said Pat.

Finally, I recounted the circumstances and historical significance.

'Leave it with me, I'll get back onto you,' and the line went dead.

Minutes later, he rang back and explained that he had contacted the director of antiquities at the National Museum, who confirmed that if the missing artefacts were as described then they were indeed priceless items of international historical significance. The pressure was now on for a result and it lay squarely on my shoulders.

'How long will it take you to finish there?' he asked.

'I couldn't say, Pat, maybe an hour and a half,' I replied, knowing that he was up to something, always playing his cards close to his chest.

'Listen, I know you always do a good job but we really need a result on this one. Are you getting any lifts? The minute you write up your exhibits let me know and I will have them rushed to the fingerprint section for analysis.'

That was how crime scene investigation worked; in the immediate aftermath of a serious incident the entire focus was on retrieving forensic evidence. I knew that this urgency would only increase as the information went up the chain of command and immediately boomerang back to where I was kneeling on the floor with the weight of expectation on my shoulders. Not needing useless requests for updates interrupting my examination, I switched off my phone.

I concentrated on everything the raiders might have touched, hoping against hope that an ungloved hand might have handled the dropped medication and perfume containers. As I dusted the cover of a Solpadeine box, the outline of a good fingerprint started to form. I smoothed the powder across the surface again and shone my torch on it.

A full outline was difficult to see due to the red background colouring but there seemed to be some detail. I peeled back the lifting tape, cautious not to wrinkle it, anchoring the box against my toolkit and carefully spreading the clear tape across the surface.

This was the most crucial part of the process as any wrinkling or movement was capable of destroying the delicate outline of the developed print. Slowly I placed my left finger on the outside of the tape and gently eased it across the surface, smoothing it more with a clean cloth. I gently peeled back the tape and watched as it lifted impressions that would be destroyed if they met any surface. I also held my breath, conscious that its moisture could be problematic. Finally I anchored the blank end of the wide tape lift to the top of my toolbox, pressing the section containing the print onto the surface of the white lift card, and it appeared smooth. Finally, I wrote up each fingerprint lift card, identifying where they were lifted from, as well as the date, time and place, and adding a small sketch, which I also documented, in my notebook. My examination was finished; head thumping with the level of concentration that it had required, I phoned Detective Inspector Pat Finlay and soon the fingerprint lift cards and submission documentation were en route to Dublin. I said goodbye to Sunniva, and continued on to the next crime scene requiring examination.

Finishing work at 6:00 p.m. that evening, as I was driving home I had the opportunity to consider the potential historical significance of the gold artefacts which had lain for so long in that peat bog. It had been a long time since 1947 but just a tiny speck in time relative to when they had been buried, and I could see how easily they were forgotten in the safe, paper-thin items just lying there inside a sheet of newspaper enclosed in an envelope.

Detective Garda Ernie Frazier was on duty at the fingerprints section in Garda Headquarters and was intrigued by the circumstances of this case, which had just landed on his desk. A fingerprint expert, his duties also entailed examining high priority lift cards submitted for analysis, especially in urgent cases such as this. Removing the fingerprint lift cards I had submitted and viewing each individually under magnification, his experienced eye quickly zeroed in on the lift from the Solpadeine box and he set to work establishing the parameters for the Automated Fingerprint Identification System (AFIS) computer system. The AFIS system is a biometric solution consisting of a computer database of fingerprint records, which is able to search and compare them to identify known or unknown fingerprints. Modern AFIS systems have the capability to search millions of fingerprint records in a short time period. All results are then manually cross checked by a fingerprint expert.

At 10:00 p.m. my phone rang. Usually when a call came from Detective Inspector Pat Finlay at that hour there was a body waiting.

'Well done, you came up with the goods,' he said, going on to describe how a positive AFIS identification hit from the Solpadeine box lift card had been linked to a suspect living in Dublin and that detectives were heading up there in the morning with a search warrant. I really hoped the artefacts would be recovered.

Then Detective Sergeant John Costello was a hands-on garda and the last of a dying breed, now a senior investigating officer, who had no truck with the layers of bureaucracy that often tried to stymie him. A former member of the Emergency Response Unit, at the time of the pharmacy heist he was responsible for crime in the garda district of Roscommon. His talent lay in his relentless drive to track even the tiniest traces of truth behind any matter that landed on his desk and he loved nothing more than getting stuck right into the middle of an interesting investigation.

At 6:00 a.m. on 28 March, the pharmacy raiders experienced the cracking sound of a front door splintering, for the second time in 24 hours, but this time it was their own. They were caught red-handed with the canvas holdalls full of the stolen property from the pharmacy. But the precious artefacts were not there and, wary that they might already have been sold on, John Costello laid his cards straight on the table.

'Lads, we don't care about this stuff, where's the jewellery?'

The criminals looked on genuinely clueless as to what he was on about.

'The gold neckband and brooches,' he clarified, but still blank faces. It turned out that they had forced open the safe and, disappointed to have found no cash, had dumped the remaining contents into skips they had passed on the way home, but which ones they couldn't now tell.

Caught red-handed in possession of the stolen medicines and perfumes, they cooperated, identifying three possibilities, each of which was full of builders' debris and household waste. The skips were delivered to the rear yard at Kilmainham Garda Station. After surviving unscathed in a bog for thousands of years, and 62 more wrapped in paper in a safe, were the artefacts now lying destroyed in a filthy skip under tonnes of rubbish? John and his team were about to find out.

Equipped with boots and old clothes they commenced their trawl, item by item, the smell at times sickening but not deterring. At one point a detective located an envelope with what appeared to be metallic nuggets, but Sunniva said an uncle had brought them home to her father from an Australian mine in the 1930s.

Another soul-destroying few hours passed and the buzz of knowing they were on the right track had worn off when something caught John's eye beneath a refuse sack, whose putrid contents had started to leak, the smell overwhelming. Lifting a concrete block from on top of it he threw the stinking bag to the end of the skip. As he bent down to take a closer look, there was a large envelope with a bundle of paper inside it. After its 4,000-year hibernation and brief exposure in 1947, the delicate gold lunula once more saw the light of day. Incredibly the gold discs were there too, no worse for wear. This was policing at its finest, quality crime scene investigation providing the result for swift, decisive detective work resulting in an outcome of worldwide historical significance.

Today they sit proudly on display at the National Museum of Ireland and their beauty and delicate craftmanship is breathtaking. Known as the Coggalbeg Hoard, they are regarded as the most significant discovery of their type ever made and hold pride of place in the museum display. The trial judge, Mr Justice Anthony Kennedy, considered the two raiders as heroes rather than villains. He was interested to hear that they had visited the National Museum to view the pieces and, recognising their background of deprivation, gave them both suspended sentences to be immediately activated should they re-offend.

I visited the pharmacy recently and was delighted to see that the new owners have kept the beautiful interior intact, only renovating the dispensary area at the rear. Sunniva Sheehan is now retired, healthy and well. When I called to her, after visiting the pharmacy, she recalled that when the case made national headlines her aunt, Lucy Carthy, almost 100 years young at the time of the raid, phoned to say that as a young woman she had been in the pharmacy the day that Hubert Lannon had brought in the lunula from the bog. Sunniva then produced a copy of Rosita Boland's book, *Ten Decades of Irish Life*, which featured an interview with Lucy aged 103 and a stunning, closely cropped black and white photograph of her beautiful face, the sparkle still clearly visible in her eyes. The last time Sunniva recalled seeing the lunula she was five years old. She couldn't explain why her father left it in the safe for so long,

Crime scene investigation work isn't all about sunglasses and glamour, as depicted on television or in cinema. As Brendan Kilty SC eloquently expressed during a captivating talk at the Percy French summer school in 2023: 'very often within the ordinary lies the extraordinary.'

# CHAPTER 8

# THE COLD FACTS OF LIFE

t was 28 December 2009 and Ireland was in the grip of its coldest freeze since 1963. Our temperate climate and mild winters made us ill-equipped to cope with the pre-Christmas snowfall, which had carpeted the country leaving roads in many areas impassable as temperatures plummeted. A remarkable satellite image showed the nation's usually green pastures and fields were now completely white.

A curse slipped my lips as I held the kettle under the cold tap only to be greeted with silence. I was on a day off, and here I was being faced with frozen water pipes, a domestic crisis that was being replicated across the land. But a cuppa made from the hot tap and slice of toast later, I was ready to try to solve the problem. And soon I was to learn that a stroke of luck had saved the day; the outside tap had not been turned off properly and the dripping water had kept it from freezing.

It was as I was feeding the garden hose through an upstairs window and into the attic as a makeshift bypass system that my phone rang. It was my colleague Garda Valerie O'Loughlin, who was stranded in Mayo due to the weather conditions and unable to make it back in time for work.

'No problem, I'll cover you,' I said as I crawled through the tight attic space with the phone jammed between my ear and shoulder, as I fed the trailing garden hose into the water tank.

'Eh, there is one thing though, Granard just called me. They have a dead body which they want us to take a quick look at.'

I rang Granard Garda Station to say I would be on the way as soon as I had collected our transport in Roscommon. I opted for the Toyota Land Cruiser 4x4, an old jeep but ideally suited to the challenging conditions. Starting it up and leaving it to thaw while ticking over, I loaded my equipment for the job ahead. A quick double-check for camera batteries and I was ready.

The four-wheel drive made light of the treacherous driving conditions, but several cars stranded along the way ensured that it still took over an hour and a half to get to Granard. Travelling through this winter wonderland, with children building large snowmen in their gardens as I passed, I pondered on how bereavement at this time of year was particularly sad. Having looked forward to an extended festive break, a family was about to be notified of the unexpected death of a loved one.

Granard's skyline took shape in the distance ahead, the church spire dominating the hillside. Powdered with heavy snow and frozen icicles standing sentry on the guttering, it looked picture postcard perfect. Bounded by Pat the Baker's on the north and The Mart on the south, Granard's east and west borders blended easily into the rural blanketed landscape.

The deceased's body was in a house on Farrell's Terrace and an aroma of bread drifted from the nearby Pat the Baker premises as I stepped out onto the road. I carefully picked my steps along the icy surface, brittle snow crunching underfoot. The undertaker's hearse was parked at a distance and stirred a memory deep within. I had always found those black vehicles sinister and foreboding, a potent symbol of the death I had feared as a child. Now I was about to make a judgement call about its next occupant. I figured there mustn't have been too much out of place if the undertaker was already in situ. I noted the time as 1:30 p.m.

Garda Phil O'Keefe of Granard Garda Station who was preserving the scene provided me with background detail. The deceased, Peter Conroy, had lived alone and had been found dead in his kitchen earlier that morning with a head injury and a lot of blood on the floor. It was explained that he drank heavily on a regular basis and his front door was often left open as it had been when the body had been discovered, which struck me as strange given the freezing conditions outside. I made a mental note to thoroughly check the locks and doors and recorded the temperature as −7°C according to the jeep's gauge. If anything, it felt even colder.

I stepped carefully along the pathway, almost slipping as I prepared to first carry out a visual inspection of the house. But before going inside, I paused short of the front door and took in the light yellow walls and white uPVC windows and doors. Then I ran a mental background check for signs of anything unusual or out of place, no matter how minor.

A quick inspection revealed no evidence to suggest forced entry on either the exterior windows or doors. Ash deposits in the front yard corner indicated that the deceased had an open fireplace. Beneath the compacted snow and ice, a concrete surface lay hidden. The porch light was on and the front door was slightly ajar. I slowly pushed open the door, which dragged on the ground, and led directly into a sitting room, in which a staircase visibly extended to the first floor. Pausing on the step to absorb the layout,

I observed a small smudge of blood on the inside door reveal and a marking pattern on the wall leading upstairs. It began high and extended about three feet wide before leaving a dripping trace down the wall and onto the skirting board. A closer examination revealed signs of sticky yolk and shell fragments at the impact site and on the floorboards immediately below. The bedroom had also been similarly targeted. That the walls had been egged immediately set off alarm bells; had local youths been terrorising this poor man living alone? I had ready access to the house so my next step was to perform an initial visual examination. Anything it unearthed would have to be considered through one lens in particular: the grim possibility that violence had been inflicted on the deceased.

Looking closer at the left-hand side of the doorway wall entering the house I noted that there was a contact bloodstain pattern. In simple terms, this means a bloody source had briefly come into contact with the unstained surface, depositing the small trace. I observed several blood drops – volumes of blood that fall or drip due to the force of gravity – on the wooden floor in front of the sofa and toward the kitchen entrance door, and could see another on the ground near the door threshold leading to where the body lay. The fire grate was full of ash and turf unconsumed by the fire. Placing my gloved hand into the ash, it felt cold, with no trace of heat. The drops of blood on the floor in front of the sofa, with a cigarette butt lying on the ground beside them, suggested that Peter may have sat there after receiving the head injury.

Quickly, I closed off such speculative promptings and noted an empty 20 Major cigarette box resting against the fire grate. When I went then to close the front door, I found it wouldn't do so with the pressure of my hand, as it dragged on the wooden floor. The only way I could close it was by applying the pressure of my body to the task. I registered this observation in my notebook at 2:18 p.m., as a possible explanation for the earlier assertion that the door was frequently left open. Then I walked into the freezing-cold kitchen, where Peter Conroy's lifeless body lay face down in the far-right corner near the back door.

The kitchen had also been used to store a pile of turf, as well as three large plastic calf feed bags of wood for the open fire. A sideboard was full of empty beer cans, on top of which stood an empty vodka bottle, assorted cider and wine bottles and some containers. The back door was secured by a piece of wood nailed to the adjacent wall.

On the far-right-hand side of the centrally located table and chair set, there was evidence of blood on the floor, with more blood to the left-hand side of the body. This suggested that Peter had been bleeding in that area for some time, while moving about. A vacant space underneath the countertop had been plumbed for a washing machine; grey feed pipes protruded from the wall. There were some visible blood drops there too, indicating that his head had been under the counter area two inches from the end wall. Perhaps he had been there, disoriented, before he died.

Peter's body lay in such a way that his head was in a corner of the kitchen, beside a barstool, very close to its base leg. The back of his head and face were stained with blood and ash. I checked his hands and arms for signs of defensive wounds and there were none. Likewise his neck and torso bore no evidence of injury. To the right of his body, on the floor, sat two buckets and a mop with two bloodstains on the handle, which suggested an attempt to mop up the blood that flowed from his head when he had hit the floor. The radiator had contact bloodstaining on its surface, two feet from the floor.

Underneath the radiator was further evidence of contact bloodstaining, suggesting that he had moved around that area as well before he died. A semicircular ash deposit marked the seat area of his jeans, consistent with the shape of the metal ash bucket, and some broken cup fragments lay on the ground in front of the sink.

Once more, I stood alone with the departed and absorbed every single detail. Silence, contemplation and absolute concentration increased my focus as I soaked everything in. Only after a prolonged period of immersion did I allow my mind to start piecing together possible scenarios.

The available evidence suggested the possibility of a fall outside the house, perhaps while emptying the ash bucket. Although I could see no blood drops on the snow outside, I visualised Peter putting a hand to his head and then to the door reveal as he entered, before sitting on the sofa, blood dropping to the floor as he lit his last cigarette.

I stood there and visualised him moving to the kitchen and releasing the cup, which broke as it hit the unforgiving tiled floor, before walking on the blood as it gathered on the ground, as evidenced by the stains on his boot soles. I saw him grabbing the mop and wiping the floor where he stood, using the handle as support before becoming weak and falling to the floor. I imagined him trying to get up but the shock of the injury and cold taking effect. Managing to rise and sit on the rim of the metal bucket before slumping back to the floor, the ash spilling and sticking to his head and face as he moved around, slowly losing consciousness. With nobody present to hear or assist, the lifeforce draining out of him.

However, I still could not discount the possibility of an assault, the evidence of egging on the living room walls and in the master bedroom demonstrating at the very least malicious vandalism. While the bloodstain patterns had not suggested a violent altercation or struggle, the signs of unwelcome visitors were causing me concern. Likewise the head wound. How and where did it happen, was it accidental or was there something more sinister at play? I decided to request that the state pathologist carry out a forensic post-mortem and explained to Garda Phil O'Keefe that the undertaker's services would no longer be needed. Photographing the scene and recording my observations in my large A4 hardback notebook, I sketched out the dimensions and layout of the kitchen and documented all of the salient details. It was soon confirmed that Dr Khalid Jaber would carry out the post-mortem at the mortuary in Regional Hospital Mullingar at 2:00 p.m. the following day and that a garda presence would be maintained overnight to ensure that the scene was preserved.

The following morning, accompanied by Sergeant Mary Mangan and Garda Ray Greenan, highly experienced colleagues from the CSI Longford office, we met with Dr Khalid Jaber at 4 Farrell's Terrace. He had only recently been appointed to the Office of the State Pathologist, and this was our first encounter with him. Introductions were exchanged and I was struck by his gentle and mild-natured manner, as well as his immaculate grooming. Dressed in a jacket, shirt and tie, a fine three-quarter-length overcoat and brown brogues, with a neatly trimmed moustache and stylish pair of rimless glasses topping off the look, the new deputy state pathologist looked every inch the television depiction of a medical consultant. Exuding a calm manner and demeanour, he listened intently as I presented my scene interpretation and outlined my reasons for calling his office.

At the mortuary that afternoon, I was assigned to take photographs of the post-mortem examination while Ray secured the samples. I paid close attention to Dr Jaber's work procedures, the most significant being that he neither took notes nor dictated his findings into a recorder. Instead he instructed me to take a lengthy series of exact and detailed photographs of every blemish and mark on the body and every stage of the post-mortem process.

As he progressed through his minute internal examination, he took particular interest in the small and double-sided wound on Peter's head, unusual because the crescent-shaped outline was not deep and, in his view, unindicative of a violent attack. As Dr Jaber cleared around the wound, he delicately shaved the hair away with a razor, exposing an opposing crescent wound measuring 2cm and curved on both sides. As we speculated about this unusual shape, its small size and very distinct pattern, I scrolled up my scene photographs of the bucket rim.

Dr Jaber silently considered the images as I enlarged them on the camera display screen, focusing on the small, curved metal segment of the bucket handle where it intersected with the holding portion on the rim. His gaze went from the wound to the photo and back to the wound. After what seemed like an eternity, he reasoned aloud that a fall on the icy surface outside the house and striking his head on this part of the bucket could indeed have accounted for the unusual pattern.

Further supporting this and adding plausibility to his theory was the blood present on the curved metal section of the bucket handle connection. Dr Jaber continued with his meticulous examination, with me photographing each stage. The post-mortem took four hours and fifteen minutes and though I was drained by the intense concentration required, the job wasn't finished yet.

Standard practice is that after a post-mortem, a senior garda of superintendent rank have a sit-down briefing with the state pathologist, where the cause of death is explained, evidence of any foul play outlined and a decision about opening a murder investigation taken. However, due to the treacherous driving conditions, a senior garda officer wasn't in a position to attend the briefing. Only Sergeant Mary Mangan, Garda Ray Greenan and I were present to hear Dr Jaber's findings.

As we waited for him to change out of his scrubs, I felt some concern that he had neither taken contemporaneous notes nor dictated his findings on a recording. My photographs were now the only formal record of the post-mortem. As soon as we began, I started writing, recording the time as 6:20 p.m. At length, Dr Jaber described his findings, thoughts and reasoning, outlining the cause of death and immediately elaborating with observations, theory and explanations. I scribbled frantically to keep pace with him, my handwriting just about keeping up with the task without the opportunity to check for legibility.

Dr Jaber described Peter Conroy as having had a weakness in the heart and stated the cause of his death as acute heart failure. He asserted that the laceration to the deceased's scalp had not been deep, and that death had not occurred from blood loss. There had been no injury to the brain, he explained, nor evidence of a fracture, although there had been discolouration inside the skull consistent with an old head injury. The scalp hematoma and tissue swelling were described as fresh but the closely situated lacerations with bridging intact had not penetrated the skull. Dr Jaber referred to the crescent-type double wound and stated that the blunt force trauma to Peter's scalp could have resulted from a fall while emptying the ash bucket, the unusual wound pattern consistent with the opposing crescent metal connection to the bucket rim. He did not consider the rib fractures as being the result of a violent attack or assault and speculated that, given the icy conditions over the past while, a fall was plausible.

Dr Jaber's findings were long and rambling and we needed to pin him down. Conscious of the absence of a senior officer, I hesitated to interrupt but it was time for clarity. I enquired if there was sufficient evidence to suggest a violent death and whether or not we had a murder on our hands. Dr Jaber reaffirmed that, based on his discovery of a large and dilated heart and the presence of hypertension and sclerosis of the arteries, Peter Conroy had died from acute heart failure. He speculated that this might have been slow given that the deceased was not a hardy man and that there had been the start of hypothermia on display. As he rounded off his summary, I reviewed my notes, relieved that I could read them and satisfied that they were an accurate and contemporaneous account of what we had been told.

With the deputy state pathologist decreeing that the death was not suspicious, the preserved status of the scene was lifted and

134

no further examination took place. As there was no murder case, our involvement in the investigation as crime scene investigators was concluded. The local gardaí submitted an inquest file to the Coroners' Office, which included statements from those involved in the case, such as the last person to see the deceased alive, the one who found the body, the doctor who pronounced death, the investigating gardaí and so on.

On 17 June 2010, Dr Jaber submitted his 19-page official post-mortem report, accompanied by a toxicology report, which indicated an absence of any alcohol in Peter Conroy's blood. Although these findings did not correlate with the background information from the scene (which showed evidence of a large number of empty alcohol containers), a mix-up at the State Laboratory where the blood and urine samples were tested was extremely unlikely. Procedures for the continuity of samples once received at the laboratory were virtually watertight.

Dr Jaber's post-mortem report differed from the detailed contemporaneous notes I had taken in one crucial manner: there was no mention of acute heart failure. The primary causes of death were now being presented as (a) blunt force trauma, (b) chronic alcoholism, (c) atherosclerotic and hypertensive cardiovascular disease, (d) maltoma (lymphoid tissue malignancy of gastrointestinal and bronchial tracts) and (e) hypothermia. The classification of blunt force trauma as the primary cause of death was in direct contradiction to his findings as dictated after the post-mortem. The order and prominence of their presentation also contrasted with that account. My record specifically showed that he had offered the expressed opinion that Peter Conroy had died of acute heart failure and now his report even excluded this as a cause. I was not overly concerned, however, knowing the inquest hearing would tease out these issues and that Dr Jaber would be present to clarify and explain such discrepancies to the coroner and jury.

—◆—

I had not been asked to make a statement and as a result was not called to the inquest, which took place two and a half years later, in May 2012. The first I knew of it was a phone call from Sergeant Mary Mangan to say that RTÉ News had a piece with midlands correspondent Ciaran Mullooly outlining the family's shock and upset at the evidence presented by Dr Jaber. The inquest had recorded an open verdict and on 8 July 2012 the *Longford Leader* reported:

> The family of a north Longford man have launched a direct appeal to Minister for Justice Alan Shatter in a bid to re-open an investigation into their father's death two and a half years ago. Sixty-six-year-old Peter Conroy was discovered by a neighbour on the 28th of December 2009, in the kitchen area of his home in Granard lying face down on the floor. Investigations carried out by gardaí at the time revealed no evidence of foul play and no charges were ever brought in connection with the Ballynacargy native's death.
>
> However, at his Inquest in May, it emerged that Mr Conroy had sustained multiple bruises to both his upper and lower body, a discovery which left deputy state pathologist Dr Khalid Jaber baffled. Dr Jaber said he was unable to explain

how Mr Conroy might have received the injuries, especially as toxicology results showed the pensioner had no alcohol in his system at the time. 'I have seen cases of alcoholism. These cases would normally equate to where an alcoholic had a very high blood level on him. In this case, I don't have supportive evidence to explain to me why he (Mr Conroy) sustained the cuts on the back of his head and caused his bleeding. (This) is because he doesn't have acute alcoholism on him. For me, it is a concern why he sustained an injury.'

Two months on, two of Mr Conroy's daughters, Sandra and Aisling, spoke exclusively to the *Leader* about their concerns and for their father's case file to be re-examined. Pointing out how her father had spent Christmas with another of his daughters, Tara, an emotional Sandra told of how the family are still searching for answers two and a half years later. 'Apart from a tingling foot and bad cough, he was in reasonable health. That's what we can't understand' said Sandra. 'We were told that he had a terrible gash to the back of his head and that there was a lot of blood, but we just thought he had fallen.'

Ms Conroy's sister, Aisling, also revealed her father spoke openly about how he had been the victim of anti-social behaviour in the past, leading to his decision to move home. 'He had to move from Colmcille's Terrace to Farrell's Terrace as windows were always being broken. Even the panels of the door were kicked in,' she said. Both during the inquest and in the weeks since, the family have held talks with senior gardaí in a last-ditch attempt to re-open their father's case.

Members of the family likewise held a meeting with Longford–Westmeath TD James Bannon on Monday evening. It's a move which all four of Mr Conroy's daughters hope will force government leaders into a re-think on the issue. 'He didn't die of a heart attack,' added Sandra. 'If he was drunk and stumbled, we would say fair enough but he didn't. We just want to know what happened to him. We want the case re-opened. We want closure.'

I received an urgent request from the chief superintendent for an immediate comprehensive report regarding my role at the scene, which I submitted by return, outlining the sequence of events and my detailed recording of Dr Jaber's briefing following the post-mortem. On 8 November 2012, I was detailed to meet with the family at Granard Garda Station to explain my findings at the scene. Naturally they were devastated at the testimony from Dr Jaber at the inquest and appalled that there was to be no garda murder investigation.

When I reviewed my notes and scene photographs in advance of meeting them, I realised that there was potentially a simple explanation for Dr Jaber's inability to account for Peter having fallen in the absence of alcohol as a contributory factor: he had no notes to refer to. When compiling his post-mortem report six months after the event, all he possessed was the photographic material I had supplied him with. I speculated that by the time came for evidence at the inquest hearing he had no recollection of the treacherous icy underfoot conditions he referred to several times while briefing us after the post-mortem. That I had not been called as a witness at the inquest meant there had been no evidence available to assist the coroner with certain crucial background details, which might have saved the family some worry, heartache and distress.

The atmosphere was tense as I walked into the superintendent's office at Granard Garda Station, accompanied by Sergeant Mary Mangan, almost four months after the inquest revelations. Superintendent Ian Lackey sat at his desk as we exchanged introductions with Peter Conroy's daughters. I sympathised with them on their father's loss and assured them that I had thoroughly examined the scene. I explained how both the gardaí and undertaker had been present upon my arrival and my reasoning for sending them away was that I wanted the state pathologist to carry out a forensic post-mortem. I explained that I had not been happy with the fact that the walls of the house had been egged, and that I had concluded that the safest course of action was to have a forensic post-mortem.

Outlining my observations at the scene, I referred constantly to my detailed notes. They listened intently to my serious concerns about the egged walls, the wound on Peter's head and Dr Jaber's findings regarding the cause of death. I read directly from the notes I had taken as the deputy state pathologist briefed us, following the post-mortem. They were very upset to hear such vivid detail and I paused occasionally to allow them to absorb the implications. Finally, I told them that my scene and post-mortem photographs were available for examination, and suggested they have a legal representative view them on their behalf. They appeared satisfied that the necessary investigations had been comprehensively carried out and relieved to finally have some specific explanations to consider.

Dr Jaber resigned with immediate effect from the Office of the State Pathologist on 26 November 2013 following a dispute with the Department of Justice and his insistence that he had acted professionally at all times. Controversy had arisen in other cases as well regarding testimonial differences between post-mortem briefing assessments and the content of the eventual reports. The *Irish Times*, for example, reported on 29 July 2015 that Dr Jaber had given an opinion at a murder trial, on one such cause of death substantially at odds with the charges alleged:

> President of the Court of Appeal Mr Justice Seán Ryan said the appeal arose out of the then deputy state pathologist Dr Khalid Jaber's 'crucial' evidence in the case. The defence submitted that they were presented with conclusions on the cause of death that had not been notified to them in advance.
>
> The case against Coughlan was that he had forced Mr Greene into the river where the man died by drowning. 'That was the case that was made.' However, Dr Jaber also produced an opinion that Mr Greene had been strangled before he got into the water, the judgment stated.
>
> It was 'not satisfactory' that that was given 'for the first time in the witness box when the pathologist was giving evidence in the course of an important murder trial', Mr Justice Ryan said. 'In fairness to the prosecution … it came as news to the prosecution, as much as to anybody else,' Mr Justice Ryan said. The prosecution dealt with this 'as best they could,' the judgment stated, and the trial judge made 'heroic efforts' to ensure fairness would ensue.

Taking detailed notes at a crime scene is one of the most critically important tasks of any investigator. This is something I absorbed in the early days of my garda career, and had I not recorded Dr Jaber's briefing in such a detailed way, the Conroy family would have been left in limbo. Despite his senior public position and status, experience and a sixth sense that the deputy state pathologist's lack of notes might be problematic led to me feeling compelled to record his every word in writing. I dread to think of the heartbreak that would have ensued had the family not received a credible, documented explanation as to why there was no murder investigation.

# CHAPTER 9

# MYSTERIES OF THE UNEXPLAINED

n the early 1980s, a weekly magazine called *The Unexplained: Mysteries of Mind, Space & Time* held a particular fascination for 12-year-old me, recounting strange tales of manlike beasts such as Bigfoot and the Yeti, and providing grainy long-distance photographs as conclusive evidence of their existence. Even our very own Lough Ree Monster merited a brief mention, signalling a renewed interest in the dark mysterious waters on our doorstep. A spate of tragic drownings during that period added to the foreboding allure of this lake in our midst, and my friends and I often wondered about the strange sights which might be revealed were it somehow ever to be drained.

The mysteries of space, including the possibility of time travel through black holes, featured regularly in the magazine, and accounts of real-life encounters with unidentified flying objects (UFOs) were frequently chronicled. Tales abounded of the mysterious Bermuda Triangle, especially the disappearance without a trace in 1945 of Flight 19, a squadron of five Avenger torpedo bombers and the Mariner flying boat that launched to search for them.

Many instalments of *The Unexplained* were devoted to the grisly spectre of horrific deaths, one issue in particular dealing with 'spontaneous human combustion', the notion that a fire had started within the body of a victim without an apparent external source of ignition. This subject held particular fascination in Victorian England, with published accounts dating back hundreds of years.

The phrase was actually first used by Paul Rolli, a fellow of the Royal Society, in a 1746 article concerning the death of Countess Cornelia Zangheri Bandi. I can still recall looking in horror at a reproduced photograph in the magazine of the partly charred remains of a lady sitting in a chair with the rest of the room mysteriously intact, the narrative behind such occurrences being that they could occur randomly and to anybody, a terrifying proposition indeed.

Little did I know that such fire scenarios, as speculated upon in the magazine, would become a staple of my working life many decades later. While many mysteries were encountered during my time as a crime scene investigator, most had a logical explanation. During the fatal fire investigation section of our forensic training, we were warned of the perils of making any such conclusions and it was made clear to us that supposed cases of spontaneous human combustion were almost always caused by some form of ignition source, often a cigarette, candle or body part close to a fire, which caused the fully incinerated effect of some of the body while also leaving certain limbs intact.

◆

In September 2011, Michael O'Fathartha was found burned to death in his home in Galway. No accelerants were found at the scene and an investigation determined that the open fireplace in his home was not the cause of the fire. At the inquest, the garda crime scene investigator and senior fire officer both said that they could not explain how he came to be burned to death. Ultimately, west Galway coroner, Dr Ciaran McLoughlin, concluded, 'This fire was thoroughly investigated and I'm left with the conclusion that this fits into the category of spontaneous human combustion, for which there is no adequate explanation.'

However, there was little evidence from the fire scene to support this proposition, especially as temperatures of more than 2,000 degrees Fahrenheit would have been required for a human to self-combust. After attending a different post-mortem examination around the same time, our conversation turned to the spectacular headlines which had reached international shores. Dr Marie Cassidy raised an eyebrow as to the finding of spontaneous human combustion, her vast experience explaining instead how the body could become like an inside-out candle, the person's clothes being the wick and their body fat the wax resulting in a very slow burn, often after the deceased had already died of natural causes.

◆

Often, though, circumstances conspired to complicate the unravelling of the mystery and sometimes the associated behaviours defied explanation. A year earlier, on 13 March 2010, I myself had received a request to attend the scene of a fatal fire, which was unusual in that the house was fully intact but the deceased had been partially burned. Approaching the rural cottage set back from the roadway in the townland of Slatta, Kilglass, County Roscommon, I could see that it was in reasonable condition and while perhaps in need of some tender loving care, its pleasant setting compensated for any dereliction. I parked the van by the roadside, a patrol car blocking my access, and was introduced by two gardaí to the deceased Paul Merity's daughter Paula and her partner Daniel. Sympathising on the loss of her father, I explained that my role was to ensure that there had been no foul play involved. Paula spoke in candid terms about her dad.

'He very much was a loner and suffered from an alcohol problem. He had been living here for the past few years.'

She also referred to his severe respiratory condition, exacerbated by a heavy smoking habit.

'I became concerned that he hadn't answered his phone for a few days,' she said. 'He had attended a hospital appointment on the Wednesday.'

Entering Paul's home for a visual internal inspection, I noticed that it was laid out in a traditional country cottage style, a large open fireplace dominating the main room. Here and there on the floor lay bags of empty drink cans and bottles, confirming Paula's description. Although somewhat untidy, the house did not have the extensive squalor I had often associated with similar circumstances.

This appeared to be the home of a very well-read man. Filled with assorted newspapers, magazines and books covering a wide and varied range of subjects, evidence of a natural curiosity, there were no signs whatsoever of burning or internal smoke damage within the room itself. Yet spread across the front of the open fireplace lay the body of Mr Paul Merity displaying all of the classic signs of what the childhood magazine termed a 'spontaneous human combustion'. His body was severely burned in a number of areas, his legs consumed, and yet his feet and shoes remained intact. His knees touched the grate and his body was fully contained inside a metal fender, which extended around the fireplace. A chair located to the side displayed signs of charring.

My attention now was sharply focused on ensuring that there was no evidence of violence having been inflicted on Paul, in advance of his demise. Once again it was time for intense concentration, silence and keen observation. Could there be any indication of violent activity, any sign that Paul had been subjected to an assault or that intruders had forcibly entered his home? When standing alone with a body in such difficult circumstances, my thoughts were entirely with the family and the duty I felt to them. I felt this even more keenly, having spoken to and sympathised with Paula outside the house. There was no time for any squeamishness. I was determined to ensure that I conducted my scene examination methodically, efficiently and professionally.

As I crouched down to take a closer look at the body, the door from the kitchen opened behind me. Assuming it was one of the gardaí, I continued my detailed concentration without looking up.

'Sure this is straightforward, many's the time I dealt with the like of it,' spoke the intruder with an authoritative tone.

I turned to see a man in his mid-seventies. 'Sorry, you can't be in here, please leave,' I said, wondering how he had gained access.

'Relax, would you, I know this man well,' he continued.

Walking towards the front door I ushered him out, 'Please leave.'

'Who's that fella?' he asked the garda outside.

'Ciaran Prior,' she answered respectfully, 'he's our crime scene investigator.'

'Is he a son of Prior, the detective sergeant? the man persisted.

'I don't know,' came the discreet reply. 'Indeed, that's who he is.'

When he walked away, the garda confirmed a hunch I had about this man's identity.

'That's the infamous Tom Tully, the retired sergeant formerly in charge of Boyle Garda Station. He's after sickening the poor daughter with stories from his glory days and how he sorted out a government minister. So inappropriate.'

I, too, was mortified at his insensitivity shown to Paula, the deceased's daughter, especially in light of a recent newspaper article I had read praising him as a man of honour, virtue and bravery for having resisted political interference during his garda career. Much loved by his family and well-respected among his community, opinion had been divided between those who had worked alongside him.

Content that I could now focus unhindered on my work, I photographed the cottage interior, sketched the room and location of the body, and set about making detailed notes recording my observations. As Garda Pat O'Grady watched on, I enlisted the assistance of the undertaker Aidan Tully. With his help I gently rolled the body over to make sure that the underside had no unexpected non-fire-related wounding. As I was doing so, I heard the door opening behind us and saw it was Tom Tully again.

'For f**k's sake, Pat, will you get that bollocks out of here?' I said incredulously, the earlier insensitivity to Paula still in mind. I completed my duties without further obstruction, satisfied that there was no evidence of foul play. It would be up to the hospital pathologist to ascertain the cause of death, but there would be no murder investigation.

Preparing to leave, I sympathised once more with Paula and assured her that there was no evidence to suggest that any violence had been inflicted on her father. The later post-mortem report confirmed that Paul had died from natural causes and that, thankfully, he had not suffered. All of the burn injures were sustained after death, his clear airways and lungs indicating death had occurred beforehand.

Loading my camera and equipment in through the van's side door, I heard a noise behind me. This time Tom Tully was on a mission and a different form of spontaneous human combustion was about to be unleashed. It took the form of anger, righteousness and insult and was directed squarely at me.

'I'm going to sort you out; nobody calls me a bollocks and gets away with it. I've seen your type before in the job and I've sorted them out, and I'll sort you out too,' he ranted.

I looked on bemused, wary that he was potentially trying to provoke me into a physical confrontation.

'You think you're the hard man, don't you?' he continued, 'you haven't heard the last of this.'

'You know nothing about me,' I replied.

He jabbed his finger in my chest. 'You called me a bollocks and nobody gets away with that.'

As much as I felt like obliging him with a physical confrontation, I had been in many throughout my frontline policing years and knew how easily an escalation could occur. I badly wanted to tell him to mind his own business with the usage of distinctly ungentlemanly language, but instead I bit my tongue and said, 'What you heard was a private remark to a colleague to have you leave the scene. If you were offended, I apologise.'

'You think that will stop me, do you?' he returned.

I'd had enough. 'I'm not listening to you; if you have a problem with me, take it up with GSOC' (the Garda Síochána Ombudsman Commission).

Then I closed the door and drove off carefully, making sure he was clear of the van, but not before he gave the side of it a good thump. Shaking my head as I drove down the road, I pulled in at a nearby farm entrance and, before continuing to my next call, made a note of everything Tom Tully had said and how he had acted.

The following Monday morning, I received a call from a former colleague at Castlerea Garda Station to say that Tom Tully had just been in and had made a formal complaint about me. The procedure from then was that the complaint would be referred to the GSOC for investigation. If they held the complaint to be relatively minor, then it would be referred back to a garda superintendent to investigate, which is what happened.

A few weeks later, I was summoned to meet Superintendent Brendan Connolly, who had been appointed as the investigating officer. Having received a notice of commencement of an investigation for discourteous behaviour to a member of the public, I was obliged to provide a written statement of evidence answering the charge. This I delivered in person to Superintendent Connolly, along with a detailed report of the circumstances. In it I outlined events exactly as they had occurred, an account that was corroborated by the statements of the gardaí present, the undertaker Aidan Tully and indeed the complainant Tom Tully himself. The investigation concluded with the GSOC confirming that I had no case to answer.

◆

On 25 March 2008, I attended a double fatality for the first time as a qualified crime scene investigator. In this case, the circumstances of death were mysterious at first viewing to say the least. It is very unusual for two people to be found dead, lying face down on their kitchen floor and my thoughts once more turned to the scourge of attacks on the elderly.

The call had come in around 11:00 p.m. that a husband and wife had been found dead in their cottage at Cleen, Knockvicar, Boyle, County Roscommon. Local shopkeepers, Cathal and Anne Beirne, had become concerned for their welfare when they hadn't collected their reserved newspaper for a few days. Calling around to check, they were shocked to see through the front window the bodies of Pat and Annie McCormack lying on their living room floor.

Set back from the roadway, the modest house had a large grass frontage, where Superintendent Thomas Commons of Boyle Garda Station was waiting for me.

'Nobody has entered the house,' he said. 'The shop owners withdrew immediately and rang us.'

This was the ideal scenario for any crime scene investigator, a pristine scene with no disturbance from first responders, even if there was an attendant audience by the roadside – neighbours, gardaí and an onlooking superintendent. As I prepared my equipment and then pulled on the white protective suit and shoe coverings, I could feel their eyes on me. An initial inspection confirmed my first impressions: there was no sign of forced entry on any of the doors or windows. I remained outside leaning against the external living room windowsill, my back to the crowd, for what must have seemed to them an eternity, as I continued to absorb the scene details.

Old cobwebs along the exterior frame indicated that it had not been opened in a long time. A pile of coal was stacked beside the range and assorted bundles of old newspapers lay around the room. The overhead light illuminated the faced-down bodies, not quite side by side, Pat's near to the range and Annie's closer to the centre of the room. There was one door, opposite to where I stood, which led into the kitchen. There, the table lay on its side, its legs facing the window, and a wooden chair was on its back on the ground. Beside it, a dinnerplate and its contents lay on the floor. Another chair was positioned directly in from the entrance door, about six inches from which lay a shoe. I could see the clear presence of blood on the floor beside Pat's face. This scene was not straightforward, and I wasn't about to rush to judgement. The fact that there was upturned furniture and the possibility of there having been a disturbance had me on heightened alert.

I photographed the room through the outside window pane, making notes about the chair against the closed door directly opposite me and recording the shoe's position. I made detailed entries with sketches of every item on the floor, including both bodies. Then, raising my eyes from floor level, I scanned the walls and room surrounds at standing height. The dim lighting made it difficult to see whether there was evidence of blood on the walls; they would need to be viewed under bright lighting. It had been Palm Sunday the previous week and a leylandii shrub branch hung from a key hanger attached to the wall just inside the door frame, dangling sideways, crossing the frame and the door at head height.

I asked Sergeant Phil Coffey to enter the house by the rear door and then open the kitchen door, slowly, so I could observe what happened as I remained outside in situ looking in through the window. I watched closely as first the palm branch moved, dipping and bending slightly as the door moved inwards but retaining its position affixed to the key rack. This could only have been placed in its location by somebody in the room while the door was shut. It might have fallen to the left as a key was placed on the key hanger, explaining its positioning across the door frame, but it would have been impossible to close the door and somehow try to manipulate the palm into position as the door swung shut. As Sergeant Coffey opened the door, the shoe and chair moved as contact was made. It was now evident that no external source had been responsible for the death of the couple: an assailant could not have exited the room and arranged the palm, shoe and chair in their resting places.

With an external source ruled out, I needed to establish whether either body had injuries and if there were traces of a violent confrontation. Now entering the room for the first time, I photographed the bodies in situ and drew further sketches of the room layout in my notebook. With the help of Phil, I turned the bodies over to see if there were any signs of inflicted violence. The blood on the floor was from the natural settling process of a face pressed against the ground (when a dead body has been left lying face down for a day or two, blood and fluid will often discharge from the mouth and nose) and there were no injuries visible on either body. Whatever had happened to Pat and Annie to cause their death, there was going to be no murder investigation. It was still a highly unusual circumstance to find two elderly people dead in this manner, side by side and face down, but there was nothing suspicious about the scene.

As I stood in the room, I noted the solid fuel range and saw that there was evidence of slight smoke staining around the room,

155

poor ventilation over the years had left traces around the upper wall area.

The following day, I attended both post-mortems at University College Hospital Galway, where state pathologist Dr Marie Cassidy studied with interest the scene photographs from the previous night. Her post-mortem examination established that Pat had died of a heart attack and Annie from carbon monoxide poisoning. Who had succumbed first would forever remain a mystery. The likely scenario was that Pat had suffered a heart attack at the shock of Annie losing consciousness from the carbon monoxide, but both had passed peacefully and together.

◆

'You'll need a mask,' said the grimacing young garda exiting the old two-storey countryside house, kindly offering me one as I gave the front exterior a quick visual once over.

It was a cold, if not quite freezing, afternoon, with a watery sun and steely-grey sky. A neighbour who hadn't seen the man for a while decided to check on him.

As was often the case with older men who resided alone, conditions inside were spartan without insulation or double-glazed windows. It often happened that scenes presented to us as being complicated in a call-out turned out to be straightforward, or vice versa. Or sometimes what seemed horrific to a young garda or member of the public presented as very mild on the scale of our own vast exposure to every conceivable type of death. Sometimes the briefings given were sparse and there was a tendency for well-meaning gardaí to present a neatly packaged

156

narrative. But despite the apparent nature of a case, I always sought to maintain an open mind, from the moment I arrived until all the facts had presented themselves. Assumptions are the most dangerous of thoughts around any death scene and, while I always welcomed helpful background information, I learned to resist any temptation to judge without having the evidence to back it up. If treated with the optimum care and attention to detail, a death scene will disclose its secrets to the crime scene investigator. It is almost like a narrative has been set down in a coded format and the crime scene investigator can unlock it step by methodical step. Cold hard facts always debunked well-meaning theories and it was up to me as a CSI to make sure I could stand over every determination I made at a scene.

The dead man was in his seventies and lived alone, I was told. Then after telling me the location of the body – upstairs – and what he regarded as desperate conditions, the young garda saw no need to re-enter the house.

Inside the house it felt colder than it did outside. As I made my way, I smelled the unique scents of death, familiar to me from countless other cases.

I did not require a mask.

Entering the kitchen and living room was akin to taking a step back in time. I doubted if anything had changed in there since the 1920s, with the kitchen table, chairs and dresser reflecting a bygone era. There was no sign of anything to indicate suspicious activity. As I climbed the stairs, I noted that, although devoid of modern insulation, the house was well-built, though paint flaked from the walls and turned corners of wallpaper sheets had started to peel with old age.

The bedroom was sparsely furnished, just an old-style bed with a metal-barred headboard, a wooden chair doubling as a bedside locker and an old wooden wardrobe serving as a general storage facility, and not just for clothes. Nothing appeared to have been disturbed.

On the far side of the bed, on the wooden floor, lay the man's remains. He was on his back. Over him, a net curtain diffused the pale afternoon light which soon would fade.

From the description provided, and the young garda's grimace behind his mask, I had expected a singularly most horrendous sight, but instead I was confronted with something which both perplexed and fascinated me in its mysterious presentation. The man was wearing just a pair of shorts, a good head of grey hair and a fine bushy beard adorning his face peaceful in repose. He looked like the traditional representation of a seafaring ship's captain. There was no sign of injury or violence, nothing to indicate a suspicious death, and his later post-mortem confirmed my findings. What I viewed though, was remarkable and something I had never seen before I never saw again. It was clear why the young garda had been spooked.

The body's breakdown had not progressed at the normal pace and the man's body was covered with what looked like thousands of fine grey hairs standing erect. In the most unusual commencement of decomposition I had personally witnessed, the process had been greatly slowed down by the cooler atmosphere inside the house and a fungal type of growth appeared to have cloned his beard, covered his body, and the surrounding floor, a poignant reminder to us all that 'Dust thou art, and unto dust shalt thou return.'

———◆———

The brutality I encountered at some incidents was quite simply beyond explanation and would always remain a mystery to me.

In 2014, the Irish TV series *Love/Hate* featured a shocking rape scene involving a broken snooker cue. It was the subject of commentary for its graphic depiction of violence. I never expected to be dealing with such a crime scene four years later, especially when the setting was not a prison landing but a picturesque rural private home.

In the small box bedroom, a single bed lay on its side, the curtains on the floor, alongside sprinkles of plasterboard dust from the pole having been pulled from its fitting. Only one small blood mark was visible on the pale wall. On the upturned bed lay a segment of curtain pole, innocuous-looking until a closer look revealed one end was jagged and splintered, and a trace of bloodstaining.

Later in court, the trial judge would describe it as 'an attack of sustained barbarism'. A father and his 23-year-old son had forced entry into the home where the lover of the younger man's mother was with her. The father, held down the victim, as the son took brutal charge of the curtain pole inflicting shocking internal injuries. The man was fortunate to survive such an attack. He underwent major surgery and required a colostomy bag for several months afterwards.

Mr Des Dockery SC explained that the father had led the assault, adding that the parent had instructed his son to 'do the bastard' during the 3 a.m. attack. At the son's trial, the judge said, 'It is hard to imagine how the accused could act in such a vile, sadistic, vicious, cruel and barbaric way', and praised the victim for his 'tremendous fortitude and resilience', adding that it was abundantly clear that he was totally innocent of any wrongdoing. While the assailants received lengthy prison sentences, it is clear from his victim impact statement that the psychological trauma inflicted on the victim long outran the sentences served.

> I now find myself a different man. I have lost the confidence that I had. I have a completely different social life. I will not engage with strangers; particularly females I don't know. I find myself afraid to make decisions. I hardly ever socialise at all. I've had no sexual activity since this incident and due to the injuries I suffered, I do not know how I will manage, if at all. I have attended counselling in an effort to deal with my anxiety and to help me try and restore my confidence. I do not sleep well any more. I feel that I have lost a lot of opportunities in my life as a result of this assault.

# CHAPTER 10

# EVERY CONTACT LEAVES A TRACE

'It is impossible for a criminal to act, especially considering the intensity of a crime, without leaving traces of this presence'. These are the words of 20th century French forensic science pioneer Edmond Locard, taken from his 1931 essay, 'Traité de Criminalistique'. The insight, known as Locard's exchange principle, forms the basis for forensic science today, including all advances made since in relation to fingerprints, fibres, footprints and, much later, DNA profiling. The careful gathering of these invisible clues at the scene can enable crimes to be solved.

Interpersonal contact also leaves its own unique imprint, enriching our existence and weaving the tapestry of our daily lives. Each leaves a reciprocal trace, sometimes brief, occasionally fleeting, yet frequently indelible. Likewise, all the cold forensic proofs in the world are lame without the attendant multiple human interactions that constitute a murder investigation. Without these there would be no breakthroughs, no lights shone in dark corners searching for traces of truth, frequently leading to successful outcomes.

It would be naive to imagine that my policing interactions over the years were always positive. The very nature of the work meant that many interpersonal encounters were confrontational or tinged with an association of tragedy, leaving hurtful and long-lasting traces for those involved. In a perfect world it would have been otherwise, but sadly life does not work that way.

Few crime scenes I attended left such a deep impression in my memory as that which I attended on Saturday, 17 September 2011. A 47-year-old mother had been left for dead on the roadside.

———◆———

Earlier that day, having narrowly avoided a few soakings during our morning's work, my colleague Garda Mark Lawless and I had returned to our base in Roscommon to prepare our exhibits and accompanying paperwork for submission to the Technical Bureau's fingerprints section and Forensic Science Ireland. Meticulous record-keeping and note-taking comprised a vital part of our work. Although slow, painstaking and time-consuming, it was crucial for the integrity of exhibits being processed. The chain of custody from crime scene to Forensic Science Ireland was the backbone of any prosecution case and, were any shadow to be cast on that sequencing, an entire case could collapse.

The phone suddenly interrupted our silent work. Mark answered. A serious stabbing incident had just been reported just off the Galway Road in Roscommon town. After Mark had taken the relevant details we quickly grabbed some white protective suits and a few additional rolls of crime scene tape, we made our way the short distance to the nearby housing estate.

As a frontline uniformed garda, I was often close on hand very soon after a serious incident had occurred. However, as a crime scene investigator it was unusual to be in such proximity while the situation was still unfolding; Normally our arrival at a crime scene would be greeted by calm, the event often having occurred the day beforehand. This time though, our proximity to the incident ensured we were immediately inserted into the circumstances unfolding before our eyes. This was frontline policing at its critical stage with a life still hanging in the balance before even the paramedics had arrived.

Rounding the corner, we were confronted with the sight of Garda Sergeant Kieran Carroll on his knees cradling the head of a lady, her attractive face bloodied and distant in its expression. As she lay in the centre of the tarmacadam access roadway to the housing estate, a blue blanket shrouding her frame in the standard recovery position, the wailing of a siren drew closer. Kieran's hands gently held her head as he pleaded, 'Stay with me, Ann, stay with me.' The ashen look on her face told its own story as her focus began to fade. Glancing at Mark, I realised that he too knew the gravity of the situation. An ambulance lurched around the corner, blue lights still flashing as two paramedics rushed to her assistance, one quickly inserting an IV line in her shin and working furiously to try and revive the fading life. His colleague elevated the saline solution as the bloodstained white jacket offered no resistance to the large, angled silver blades of the scissors.

The severed material revealed multiple separate stab wounds on Ann's back and a drain tube was swiftly inserted into one. A padded cushion enabled Kieran to ease his hands away from her head and, thinking quickly, he shielded the view with a blanket to offer some semblance of privacy from the onlookers already gathering outside the tape. I lifted Ann's legs and Mark her shoulders and arms to allow the paramedics continue working as we guided her onto the stretcher and wheeled it to the ambulance, the solid clunk of the rear doors signalling the next steps in the battle to save her life. It would be touch and go.

Word came back that a suspect, Ann's 25-year-old son Paul, was in custody, having been arrested just a few yards away. We moved swiftly to erect the crime scene tape, sealing off both the roadway and house. While doing so, the sky suddenly darkened as though another downpour was imminent and we quickly scanned the roadway for items of relevance, determined to ensure that nothing of major evidential value would be at risk from the deluge. A smashed mobile phone lay in pieces on the ground alongside a light-blue sweeping brush handle, its head some yards away near the junction. Quickly covering them both with a plastic covering, we took a few swabbed samples of blood from the tarmacadam.

These additional minutes were precious as the heavens prepared to open and we were now in a frantic race against the approaching rainstorm. Heavy drops fell slowly at first, distinctive loud plops landing on the protective sheet, an advance warning of the downpour ahead. It was biblical when it finally came, floods of water pouring down the nearby drains. The wheels of the stationary ambulance were partially submerged as the flood waters gurgled down the nearby metal gulley. It was as if the skies themselves were in mourning at the sadness of the scene below.

Retreating just in time to the shelter of the house, we stood at the back doorway and carried out an initial visual inspection of the open plan kitchen and dining area. There, a couple of feet away, was the offending item, its black handle parted from the serrated blade bent from the force of the stabbing and with blood marks visible on the skewed metal. Small blood drops were dotted around the pale wooden floor and an atmosphere of deep sorrow permeated this domestic scene.

As soon as the shower had passed and the sun was drawing steam from the asphalt roadway, we returned outside to continue with our evidence-gathering. A crowd had now gathered on the far side of the crime scene tape, scrutinising each and every move we made, something we had learned to anticipate whenever the white protective suits were donned, all eyes following our every gesture. Occasionally it was preferable to delay a little before taking the crime scene's exterior photographs to give the media the opportunity to take their images first and leave, ensuring we could continue our work without being continuously tracked by intrusive camera lenses.

As Mark commenced taking photographs, I heard my name being called loudly and looked over into the expanding crowd standing on the other side of the plastic tape. Knowing the speaker to see but unable to put a name on him, I slowly approached the ashen-faced man. He turned out to be Ann's brother who lived scarcely 6 kilometres from my own homeplace. Joe was more than aware that the ambulance being still there did not augur well for his sister as generally crews stabilised their patients and then rushed them off to the hospital. In these particular circumstances there was no indication of a swift getaway, with every second onsite being crucial in the race to save her life. 'Please tell me the truth about Ann, nobody will tell me anything,' Joe insisted. 'I knew this would happen,' he continued, 'but nobody would listen.'

Walking over to the stationary ambulance, the low hum of its powerful engine still ticking over, my gut feeling sensed I would not be returning with good news. Looking through the side door, it was a hive of activity, one responder doing cardiopulmonary resuscitation (CPR) via an oxygen balloon with the other was preparing defibrillator paddles. A mechanical voice issued instructions and I turned away, feeling the eyes of the crowd on me as I walked back towards Joe. 'They're still working on her,' I offered. Please tell me the truth, how is she?' he pleaded, 'And why hasn't the ambulance moved?' 'Joe, I'm sorry, it doesn't look great,' I admitted, looking straight into his sad, worried eyes and I promised to tell him as soon as I heard anything more. A powerfully built man, his physical presence seemed to shrink visibly at this statement. 'I knew this would happen,' lamented Joe, 'I knew he would kill her. Nobody would listen to me, nobody would help.'

I left him to bring our equipment into the house so as to properly process the scene. We needed to accurately record the items of evidential value which we had covered in advance of a repeat downpour, Mark photographed each item in situ and I took measurements, making sketches and writing observations in my notebook. Joe was becoming more anxious at the absence of communication about his sister's wellbeing and once again I heard him call me over the surrounding voices. All eyes from behind the tape watched closely as my white clad figure approached him and you could have heard a pin drop as he begged, 'Ciaran, can you please tell me the truth? I'm being kept in the dark here.'

Once again, I crossed the closed-off roadway to the ambulance with the eyes of onlookers boring into my back. This time, however, the hive of activity had subsided, the ambulance staff had concluded their efforts and were in the process of silently gathering their equipment. Ann was dead. Her lifeless body lay surrounded by the visible signs of an emergency intervention such as IV line, drains, bandages and sterile packaging. One of the responders glanced at me and shook his head, despondent that despite their valiant efforts the intervention had not been sufficient. I now had to face Joe with the awful truth which he had surely suspected all along. His keen gaze followed me as I exited from the side of the ambulance and returned slowly across the roadway to the crime scene tape. No words needed to be exchanged, the sombre look on my face told him the true state of affairs. His heartfelt grief for his sister punctuated the afternoon air and the gathered crowd hushed in respectful silence. 'I'm so sorry, Joe,' I said quietly, placing my hand on his shoulder in a feeble effort to offer some small consolation. After a few seconds, he turned away from the onlookers for some small moments of privacy.

It was time to detach from the raw emotions electrifying the atmosphere and refocus on examining the scene. With Ann's son Paul in custody as a suspect for the murder of his mother, we now knew the full extent of the shocking tragedy. My sympathies for Joe's plight would be worthless if my concentration lapsed and I messed up in processing the scene, so I returned inside to Mark who had just completed the photography of the building's exterior.

We slowly and carefully walked around the kitchen visualising what had happened, the room's layout revealing its own story. Droplets of blood on the floor confirmed the stab wounds visible to us a short time ago. Marigold gloves, Cif and Domestos lined up on the counter suggested an organised mother preparing for a cleaning job she would never get to complete. The dishwasher was full with the drawer opened and it seemed as if Ann had been loading it when she was attacked from behind. She had lived in this house with Paul but had moved out when his behaviour became more erratic and dangerous, returning to clean their home after he had been there for a few weeks alone. The house's interior reflected the chaos in her son's mind, the presence of his mother reflected her love, care and concern for his welfare.

The double doors into the sitting room were ajar and I took a look around as Mark prepared the camera to visually document the scene. Glancing down at a sheaf of paperwork on the armchair, I saw on HSE-headed paper a letter addressed to Paul concerning his recent involuntary 21-day committal to residential psychiatric care under the Mental Health Act 2001. As I started to read it, a deep, sickening sensation knotted somewhere in my abdomen, the full enormity of this document's implications hitting me. Here in black and white was the cold-blooded decision of a three-person independent Mental Health Tribunal overturning Paul's earlier involuntary admission for professional treatment and deeming it safe for him to re-enter society, the eventual outcome of which was Ann lying lifeless in the back of an ambulance, her son in custody as a murder suspect, and her heartbroken brother Joe stranded behind the crime scene tape.

While Mark was reading the contents of the letter, a commotion outside the house caught my eye. Some gardaí appeared to be trying to calm Joe down and I went out to see what was wrong. He turned to me distraught.

'They won't let me see my sister, Ciaran, please let me see Ann.'

I felt compelled to act. 'Joe, it might be more upsetting for you to see Ann in this way,' I suggested.

But Joe was insistent in his resolve and I knew that he needed to see her. Once crime scene tape was erected at what was now a murder scene it was standard operating practice that nobody be allowed to enter behind it until our examination was concluded. This was to ensure the integrity of the scene and to see to it that there would be no cross-contamination.

I knew our main area of focus for the examination was inside the house where the stabbing had taken place and that Joe's decency, and integrity would allow him to leave the scene in peace if he got to see his sister's body. I was also completely satisfied that no cross-contamination would occur if I could accompany him carefully along the perimeter footpath to the ambulance where Ann lay. Across the tape, Detective Inspector Pat Finlay looked as though he had guessed what I was about to do and was not convinced it was a good idea. Approaching him, I said I wanted to bring Joe to see his sister's remains and explained that there was no issue with the scene since everything outdoors had been safely documented and protected. Trusting my judgement, he agreed to my request. I raised the tape and guided Joe to the footpath peeping above the flood water, satisfied that his wish could be acceded to and relieved to have averted a possible confrontation.

At the ambulance door I stood silently as brother and sister were reunited briefly, albeit at a distance. The exhausted paramedics stood respectfully aside and gave Joe his time with Ann albeit at a distance. Standing beside him, I put my hand gently on his shoulder as waves of grief passed through him. The crowd was silent again as we walked back together, and as I lifted the tape, a family member came forward to comfort Joe.

Back at the rear of the house, I changed into a fresh white suit and gloves. Then I returned to the ambulance before it left. Standing there in Ann's presence, I folded her jacket, top, leggings and white trainers, then placed each item into individual brown paper evidence bags. Just over an hour earlier, this caring mother was alive and well, and acting in what she considered was in her son's best interests. Little had she imagined when dressing herself that morning that by afternoon her clothing and footwear were to be neatly packaged into crime scene evidence bags by a complete stranger.

I contemplated the last look of consciousness fading in her eyes and consoled myself that at least she had been held and comforted by Kieran Carroll. I thought of her tireless efforts to be there for her son through his psychiatric difficulties, which had spiralled rapidly after a prison sentence imposed for road traffic offences. While the circumstances surrounding Ann's death seemed to be cut and dried, as crime scene investigators we could not afford to take that chance. Everything needed to proceed as normal, and I rejoined Mark inside as we got back to work of processing the scene.

Slowly, carefully and methodically I recommenced the painstaking process of retrieving, bagging and labelling every single item of evidence recovered. Each was given my 'CP' initials, followed by an ascending numbered sequence. The date, time, address and exact location of each item was also recorded on the evidence bag and in my notebook. Piece by piece, every relevant item was attended to and the large pile of evidence bags began to extend in size. Lifting the HSE's Mental Health Tribunal letter, I paused once more to read its contents, hoping that I had somehow misinterpreted it earlier and that my mind had been tainted by Joe's words. The stark truth remained self-evident; the import of its fatal directive now crystal clear. I folded it over, face down, inserted it into a document evidence bag and placed it in the corner of the room with all the others. We continued in this vein until 9:00 p.m., by which time we called it a day. As I drove home, I couldn't escape the image of Joe at the ambulance as he absorbed the shock of his dead sister's body before him. This had been a cruel event that could have been prevented, yet here we were, another family ripped apart.

An early start the following morning saw us back in the office preparing for the post-mortem that had been arranged for 11:00 a.m. at Portiuncula Hospital, Ballinasloe, County Galway. The old military adage of 'Two is one and one is none' applied to our packing of equipment, spare camera batteries, swabs, evidence bags and chargers. The last thing any crime scene investigator needed was to be caught short of supplies. On our way to the hospital we returned to the crime scene, which had been preserved overnight, and took up where we left off, the gnawing feeling that this should not have happened dominating our conversation as we continued to process the evidence.

We were more subdued than usual when we met with the deputy state pathologist Dr Mike Curtis at Portiuncula Hospital. The town and surrounding areas were in a state of shock at the previous day's awful events, and we were not immune to the collective grief. I reflected on how media coverage of violent deaths only added to the trauma for the victim's family. Soon this particular murder would fade from public consciousness and only Joe and the family would be left to grieve their tragic loss.

The mortuary at Portiuncula was a small but functional space. We exchanged friendly greetings with Dr Mike, before briefing him with the circumstances. His eyes gazed off into the distance as I told him of the contents of the Mental Health Tribunal letter found at the scene. Shaking his head resignedly, it was likely that this was not the first such fatality he had encountered as a result of similar circumstances. But by the time we finished the briefing, he was his usual ebullient and witty self, his thick Scottish accent booming around the mortuary reception area.

Returning to the cool confines of the examination room, we each attended to our respective tasks, Mark photographing the wounds and myself preparing and handling the swabs as Dr Mike took samples. It promised to be a relatively straightforward post-mortem as he sought to locate the wound that had fatally injured Ann. I stood alongside her body as Dr Mike precisely measured each wound with an angled rule, mapping the depth and directionality of the multiple stabbing wounds and recording them meticulously into his Dictaphone. There were several knife wounds clustered closely together on Ann's side and back and he was having difficulty tracking their angle due to their proximity.

'Ciaran, can I borrow your index finger for a moment? These are actually quite deep,' he said.

A slow-rising horror engulfed me as my gloved hand reached out in front of me as if in slow motion, moving frame by frame like someone was manoeuvring it with a remote control. There it rose, still attached to my arm, Mike directing me towards the wound.

'Just place your finger there while I track the probe.'

Not over the wound, not beside the wound, in the wound. I was powerless to resist, unwilling to lose face in front of the others.

'That's it, quite deep, isn't it?' Mike observed.

I watched in a state of benumbed dissociation as my gloved finger slowly hovered over, then entered into, the stab wound and descended to the bottom, the tip of my finger coming to a halt at a jagged fragment of bone, an irregularity of the rib caused by the impact of the blade. Slowly but surely I could feel the cold, clammy pressure of muscle, flesh and sinew engulfing my finger from tip to knuckle, the glove providing little barrier to the sensation. I watched as if from a distance as Mike removed the probe and spoke to the mortuary technician, his lips moving but no sound reaching me.

I looked down, perplexed. And then, suddenly, the slow motion reverted to real-time with what felt like the surge of an electrical charge, uploading the suffering and pain from Ann straight to my heart. It blasted through my body as though the seal to my invisible internal core, where I located all of these horrific scenes, had finally been breached. I instinctively recoiled, snapping my finger quickly from the wound as one would from an exposed electrical wire. Mike was still talking to the mortuary technician, Mark was reloading fresh camera batteries. Turning away, I ripped off my gloves while heading for the exit and watched with a sense of detachment and quiet curiosity as I put them into the sanitation bin. Stumbling my way towards the bathroom, I just about made it to the sink and let hot water run over the offending finger which was palpably cold. It felt as though I had somehow violated Ann's body and couldn't escape the electrical sensation which had charged through me, as though all her suffering and pain had been in that current. I soaped both hands with vigour as if trying to wash away the sensation I had felt.

Staring intently at the contours of my face in the mirror, as if for the very first time, I dispassionately observed that I was distinctly pale and drawn. I threw cold water on my face and eyes and took a few deep breaths, composing myself before returning to the post-mortem, nobody any the wiser to what had just happened. Gathering myself, I executed my tasks efficiently as if on autopilot, somehow aware that nothing would ever be the same again. How could it be after the experience I had sensed and felt?

I would not normally have made an appearance at the removal or funeral of a person whose death scene I had attended, but this was different and I felt compelled to pay my respects to Ann properly, in a dignified manner. Moreover, I needed to look Joe in the eye and offer my sympathies to him over the loss of his beloved sister. As the crowd filed by her remains, I was relieved to have this final image of Ann, where she was lying in peaceful repose. I felt the need to see her in this context after the events of the past few days.

Joe stood tall and strong despite his grief. Hoping that my presence would not be upsetting or inappropriate given what we had shared at the scene, I formally offered my condolences.

'It shouldn't have happened,' he repeated as I shook his hand and nodded in agreement before shuffling along to offer the remaining family members my sympathies.

On 23 September 2011, Paul was deemed 'unfit to attend court' and committed to the Central Mental Hospital, Dundrum, where he was assessed by two consultant psychiatrists, both of whom said that he was 'suffering from a mental disorder known as paranoid schizophrenia' and that from a clinical perspective he did not have the capacity to form the necessary criminal intent because of his mental disorder. A jury at a Castlebar sitting of the Central Criminal Court subsequently acquitted Paul on 1 May 2014 of the murder by reason of insanity and he was returned to the Central Mental Hospital. But one year later he successfully appealed his acquittal under the Criminal Law (Insanity) Act 2006 and sought a retrial so he could plead and be convicted of manslaughter by reason of diminished responsibility, thereby securing a fixed sentence instead of being under indefinite detention and treated with heavy medication.

At his retrial in February 2016, prosecution for the State, Ms Caroline Biggs SC, told of how Paul had presented from an early age with 'very significant difficulties', being diagnosed at 19 with ADHD, and again a year later with 'a borderline intellectual disability'. He took to drinking and his parents had difficulties trying to manage him. Indeed, his parents' separation a few years prior to the murder was 'largely down to their different approach to managing their son's behaviour'. At the age of 24, Paul served a ten-month sentence in prison for a number of drink-driving offences and just a year before he killed his mother he had served most of his second prison sentence in Loughan House for driving without a license or insurance.

The Mental Health Act 2001 covers involuntary admissions, which can only happen if the person concerned is unwilling to go into hospital and has one of the following conditions: (a) a mental illness; (b) a significant intellectual disability; or (c) severe dementia. One or more of the following criteria must also apply: (a) there is a risk you may cause serious harm to yourself or others; (b) your judgement is so impaired that you need treatment that is only available in a hospital; and (c) your condition could get worse if you do not get the treatment that you need.

Ms Biggs described how 'In the days and weeks prior to the killing of his mother his behaviour deteriorated even further. He had a disturbed view of his mother and tragically she was the person who loved him most. Prior to [her] death her son sent her texts threatening to cut off her fingers'. She told of how Paul had beliefs that his brother had 'planted bombs in the house' and Ann 'had put a cow in the road to stop him driving'. She outlined how in August 2011, 21 days after having been involuntarily admitted to the psychiatric unit in Roscommon University Hospital, a mental health tribunal reviewed Paul's case and found he did not fulfil the criteria to be detained in a mental hospital. This was not the only systems failure in this tragic case. Five days before she died, gardaí received a phone call from Ann who said her son had threatened to shoot her and asked would they have him committed, there was no available doctor, resulting in her being advised to ring her G.P. early on the Monday morning. The court also heard of how Paul told his friend, after picking up a black-handled knife, 'This is what I need and I'm going to butcher my mother.'

The jury agreed on a unanimous verdict of not guilty of murder by reason of insanity after deliberating for just over an hour and a half. Mr Justice Hunt then addressed them saying, 'You decided the verdict with great care and detail. It's a legally correct verdict on the evidence and a humane verdict. Mr Henry is a very unwell man, and it would be inhumane to treat him as a criminal. It is 100% likely he will be committed to a place where he will be safe.'

Each time now that I meet Joe we chat, but the tragic events of September 2011 hang unseen in the air above us. Soon again I will bump into him and the whole process will replay for both of us, the talk small but the impact of that day still looming large. I'm sure Joe feels it too.

# CHAPTER 11

# DEAD MAN WALKING

The street sign for Rue Noyal Chatillon conjured up the leafy surrounds of a beautiful Loire Valley village. I could easily have been there, listening to the dialects and people watching in autumnal sunshine from a chic French sidewalk café, before going to a bistro for some tasty and delicate cuisine.

Colleague Garda Valerie O'Loughlin snapped me out of my daydream as she opened the passenger door of our crime scene investigation van, an unmarked Ford Transit Connect, and sat in beside me, with the update that the council workmen would be delaying us for at least a few minutes longer. The cold reality was Longford on a street named in honour of its twinned Brittany town, precisely 1,428 kilometres away. It was a freezing November morning in 2016 and pangs of hunger from an empty stomach were starting to register.

A toasted sandwich and a hot pot of tea in our regular café would have to do.

Earlier that morning, we had received our usual log requests of crime scenes to be examined throughout the day. We often were provided with minimal information by investigating gardaí, but having completed our customary precautionary scan of the PULSE computer system, we had found nothing unusual about any of the requests. The request that took us to Longford was to examine a criminal damage incident at the Annally Court apartment complex where Rihards Lavickis had reported his window having been smashed. Our brief was to see whether forensic evidence could be retrieved from the scene, where previous incidents had also occurred.

As I inched the van as close as I could to the stairwell entrance of the apartment block, needing easy access to our crime scene equipment, Valerie grabbed her notebook and got out.

'I'll take a look at it, you hang tight,' she said, as the door slammed shut and she faded from view in my passenger door mirror. No. 2 Annaly Court was part of a duplex apartment complex located on the first-floor level over Grafton Court, the street I had reversed down. The apartments were accessed via a concrete stairway from a street-level recessed alleyway. The stairway faced back towards the street with the ground floor shops and business premises visible upon turning from a small landing and ascending one step onto the first-floor access area. Valerie later recounted the seemingly benign sequence of events:

I walked back down the street from where I had left the van and turned right into the recessed alleyway. As I walked towards the stairs, I heard and sensed someone approach me quickly from behind. As I turned and took the first few steps I saw that a male aged approximately 30 years, a foreign national, had gained on me and I stepped to one side to let him pass. He paused for a moment and looked at me as he approached the step, and I asked him if this was the access to Annaly Court and he mumbled something at me. I paused for a moment and then followed up the stairs, he turned left

184

out of my line of vision and I heard a door slamming shut. As I too turned left, there was no sign of the man and I saw the damage that we had been tasked to examine. The front window of Number 2 Annaly Court, the first apartment to the left of the stairwell, had been broken with pieces of glass visible on the floor area of the access balcony, a safety railing bordering its full length. I initially could not see into the apartment as the curtains were pulled. There was a clothes dryer and chair on the shared access balcony outside. I rang the doorbell a number of times and got no answer. I then knocked on the door and called out but again got no response. I then discreetly pulled the thick net curtains open and again called out as I craned my neck through the window frame and looked into the room. I could see that a wooden chair lay on its side in this living room, the only indication of disturbance. I collected a sample of broken glass from the front window and packaged it in a plastic evidence bag and photographed the exterior and access balcony.

While this was happening, I was in the van, writing up our notes from crime scenes visited earlier. When Valerie returned it was approximately 12.30 p.m. and time to break for lunch at The Courtyard Café, where we enjoyed our usual friendly welcome and chat with Teresa, who served us the eagerly anticipated BLTs. When she returned to top up our teapot, she asked whether we had heard anything about an incident in progress at the nearby shopping centre. A customer had told her of a big commotion there, and that gardaí and an ambulance were both present. Just then, our work phone rang. Detective Garda Damien McGovern informed us there had been a serious stabbing incident outside Tesco on the Rue Noyal Chatillon and that things didn't look great for the victim. This type of understatement was common when describing such incidents, perhaps to help retain an atmosphere of calm during the initial urgent chain of communications that such matters required. We continued with our lunch knowing that we could not start our examination at this early stage and the likelihood being that it would be quite some time before we could eat again. We commended Teresa that her information-gathering was superior to our own and she wished us well on our way.

The initial stages surrounding a serious incident were always filled with disbelief at what had just happened. Yet years of attending such events had provided a certain immunity from the shock, no matter how upsetting the scene. Wearing that white crime scene investigation suit also placed us apart. A hushed silence would grip the air as onlookers absorbed events and I often felt like an outsider intruding on their shock as they watched us approach, unsure as to whether they should move on or not. They would stand huddled in groups, talking quietly among themselves as shock and bewilderment were replaced by those most basic of human traits, curiosity and the instinct to help. Those who had witnessed the actual incident or its aftermath would come forward to assist by giving their account of what they had seen.

When gardaí first arrive at a crime scene, they take immediate action to preserve the scene. The crucial thing is to ensure that the area concerned remains unchanged, thereby enabling a proper examination of the scene. By the time we were back on Rue Noyal

Chatillon, the street name was almost obscured by the crime scene tape, which had been pulled across the roadway to prevent traffic and pedestrians moving and thus destroying any evidence such as blood stains on the surface. Its loose tail end was blowing repeatedly against the sign's metallic surface. Access to Longford Shopping Centre was closed off and a crowd of shocked onlookers had gathered.

I parked our crime scene van right up against the tape to allow access to our equipment through its sliding door. We stepped onto the roadway, where there was little noise save for the fluttering plastic tape, its 'Crime Scene Do Not Enter' command now twisted in reverse. I spoke with Detective Garda Damien McGovern and Sergeant Enda Daly, both experienced investigators, who pointed out the exact area between Longford Shopping Centre and Grafton Court where the stabbing was believed to have taken place. Traces of blood on the path were just about visible; I could make out a few drops from where I stood. The victim had walked around the corner and entered the shopping centre, passing the pharmacy, fruit and veg shop and onwards towards the access corridor to the centre's toilets. There he had collapsed on the ground, the severity of his injuries taking their toll. Exercising caution about the possible extent of the scene, I decided to extend the tape a bit further down the street. The sky was overcast but fortunately for us there was no sign of rain.

Stepping out the route the victim had taken, I counted 57 long strides before reaching the point of his demise. Seeing CCTV cameras, I asked whether anybody had yet looked at the footage. The angle of the corner camera just under the eaves suggested it would be touch and go as to whether it had captured the incident, but the shopping centre manager immediately arranged access to the recordings. CCTV has often been considered as an infringement on civil liberties, Orwell's Big Brother surveillance state come to pass, but the current trend of sharing our lives across social media represents a potentially even greater self-inflicted challenge to privacy. Viewing footage in advance of a crime scene examination is a priceless time-saving resource. It would be of huge assistance in managing our investigation if we could know for certain where exactly the incident had taken place, and view in real-time the unfolding sequence of events. Moreover, news of an early arrest as a result of information gleaned from CCTV could help allay the public's fear.

On our way to view the CCTV, we passed through the area where the injured man had collapsed, now preserved and sealed off with crime scene tape. This side of the shopping centre was silent except for the distant hum of activity from the entrance to Tesco, which had remained open. A tattered black t-shirt and Hugo Boss hoodie lay on the ground near the entrance to O'Hehir's café, with blood staining also visible on the ground, alongside the familiar packaging and bloodied paper towels left by the emergency medical personnel. I observed a blood contact mark on the right-hand side of a partially descended roller door shutter leading to the toilet area and thought of the stark realities of this incident, everything frozen in time awaiting our examination.

Detective Sergeant Keelan Brennan was already in the manager's office with CCTV footage primed to the relevant segment. Word had come through that the ambulance had stopped a few miles into its hospital journey to allow personnel provide medical attention. This did not bode well. Viewing the soundless footage together, it was somewhat surreal to see people going about their everyday business before a sudden explosion of violence filled the screen. We watched the injured party Akadiusz Czajkowski walking on the footpath towards the shopping centre as another man entered the frame, ran across the road and attacked him, his right arm rising and making contact with the body.

The silence of the footage and its visual clarity made it seem strangely innocuous, the knife not fully visible because of the camera angle. Replaying the footage, Valerie leaned forward, focusing intently on the violent scene.

'That's the fella who came up the stairs behind me at Anally Court, I spoke to him.' Her voice trailed off. The stabbing on the screen had taken place seconds earlier, just beyond our line of vision, as Valerie had been walking towards the apartment stairwell and I reversed the van into position.

As we recounted our attendance at the broken window scene, notification came through that the victim was dead and Detective Sergeant Brennan quickly marshalled his troops.

'Get down to the apartment at 2 Annaly Court and lift Rihards Lavickis if he's there, make sure nobody leaves until we get a search warrant.'

Lavickis was now the prime suspect for the brutal daylight murder of Akadiusz Czajkowski.

It was rare that the pieces of a murder investigation fitted together so seamlessly and into an almost perfect sequential order, so this was a time for extreme diligence. Experienced murder investigation detectives attested that an open mind was essential until all of the available evidence was gathered. We left the manager's office to continue our crime scene investigation and the detectives went to obtain the search warrant for the suspect's residence and secure the murder weapon.

On the way, I couldn't help thinking of our uniform. It differed from standard garda issue, consisting of a simple black polo t-shirt, navy tactical pants, boots and a navy casual civilian jacket. The informal look afforded some privacy to the people we encountered, allowing us to make a personal connection with them while ensuring they felt listened to and that their case was being taken seriously. But before then, it never occurred to me that it might protect us as well; Valerie's nondescript clothing may well have saved her life. Only moments after violently knifing a man to death in broad daylight, adrenaline pumping through his veins, breathless after his murderous exertion and concealing a bloodied knife, Rihards Lavickis had despite all this detected no threat from the blonde lady on the stairwell. Not only that, but she had placed her head through that broken window to view the room within while the murderer stood in the hallway, knife in hand. Had he encountered her in garda marked uniform, the outcome could have been decidedly different. Death had Valerie firmly in its sights but thankfully it was not to be her time.

It was now our job to thoroughly examine both outside and inside the shopping centre where the deceased had collapsed. I accompanied Valerie back outside to speak with Garda Daniel Lynch who was preserving the scene and explained that we would begin by photographing the location, conscious of the blood on the path and roadway area just inside the crime scene tape. Having viewed the CCTV footage, the outdoor location and the interior area where Akadiusz had collapsed, we were satisfied that this was a straightforward murder investigation scene without any complicating factors. The prime suspect had been identified and would shortly be apprehended and the murder weapon recovered. There appeared to be nothing to prevent us from processing the scene efficiently and allowing the road and shopping centre to return to normal.

The fly in the ointment was to be an internal one. When introducing myself and Valerie as members of the crime scene investigation unit to Inspector Bláithín Moran from Longford Garda Station, she said that Superintendent Jim Delaney, attending a conference with the head of the Garda Technical Bureau at Garda Headquarters, had asked his counterpart for a Technical Bureau team to conduct the investigation and instructed her that we would not be required.

'Are you serious?' I asked. 'We've already commenced a visual examination of the crime scene, looked at the CCTV footage and are ready to proceed. It'll be dark by the time they arrive from Dublin and the chaos caused by the street and shopping centre restrictions will only be aggravated.'

Inspector Bláithín Moran was unwilling to call the superintendent for clarification so, not wanting an argument in full view of the gathered onlookers, I choked down on my anger at this slight on our professionalism, integrity and honour and we removed our van and equipment and retreated.

'If they think that we're arriving back here tonight in the dark when Dublin won't come, they can go and f**k off,' I fumed.

'Wait and see,' agreed Valerie, 'they'll be back with the tail between the legs before long.'

At 5:00 p.m. we received the call from Sergeant Mary Mangan, who explained that Superintendent Delaney had now given a direct order for us to return to carry out a full forensic examination of the crime scene. My choice of language down the phone line does not need repeating here as I continued to vent my frustration at the internal bureaucracy. But any petty anger or slight I felt paled into insignificance when measured in the light of the murder investigation, so we returned to Longford with work to do. It was now dark and our job was so much more difficult. The chaos of the road closure was obvious from the traffic tailback as we inched slowly through the town. The external scene was still being preserved by Garda Daniel Lynch. Number 2 Anally Court was also classified as a crime scene, the murder weapon having been discovered there in the interim and the prime suspect Rihards Lavickis arrested.

We were joined by our colleague Garda Mark Lawless as we dressed in white personal protective suits, foot coverings and latex gloves to begin an immediate examination of the inside of Longford Shopping Centre. The first duty was to record the scene as it presented, the photographs later giving a judge and jury a clear idea of the actual scene itself and providing necessary clarity. Garda Paul Connolly was preserving the space and Mark photographed where Akadiusz had collapsed and the area leading to the toilets. We took possession of the dead man's clothing and carefully placed them in large paper evidence bags, before labelling and packaging them.

I took detailed notes and sketches in my notebook as we collected the evidence knowing that, while no works of art, trial judges placed great value on these contemporaneous notes. I noted each item that we examined before crouching onto one knee and opening my CSI kit box to take out a handful of fresh swabs. I double-checked to ensure that the date stamps were current before twisting open the one-centimetre-depth plastic lid which broke the seal and released the attached swab for use. Such a swab looks like a long Q-tip with a similar cotton type bud, though smoother at the end of the stick for collecting the sample, and similar in size to a standard unused HB pencil.

The bloodstains on the floor were starting to harden now at the edges, a potential health and safety concern. As the blood dried it became hard and brittle and when a swab was dabbed in it, the flexible stem could flick tiny fragments into the air. I concentrated on those patches of blood, which were still damp, a slight touch with the tip of the swab providing an ample amount for analysis. Then I inserted the swab back into its container tube and popped it into a plastic tamper-proof evidence bag. Having completed our tasks, we left the internal scene and entered the sealed off roadway outside the shopping centre at Rue Noyal Chatillon, which was still being preserved. I observed the blood droplets on the footpath on the approach to the Grafton Court area and we placed numbered markers beside each as Mark photographed them. We repeated the earlier process, opening a sealed swab and dipping the tip through each blood droplet before numbering them as per the markers. The likelihood was that this blood belonged to Akadiusz, but experience had shown that in a frenzied stabbing such as this the culprit can also sustain injuries, leaving a profile which would link him forensically to the scene. Again, I took detailed notes as we continued this painstaking process until we had secured our samples. The darkness meant there was little more we could do; our examination was finished for the evening and we retired to Longford Garda Station for a conference.

We were back at 7:15 a.m. the following morning, the crime scene having been preserved overnight. Mark again photographed the area in natural light before we went to the suspect's home at No. 2 Anally Court, which was being preserved by Garda Denise Dockery, who we found thawing out after a long night in the cold. This is the unglamorous but crucial side of policing that few see – ensuring that a scene remained intact.

The suspect had been arrested there in his house, the murder weapon discovered underneath a wardrobe kickboard. To put it very politely, the two-storey duplex apartment was poorly maintained. Downstairs was a kitchen/living area to the rear and a front sitting room with a stairs leading up to three bedrooms and a bathroom. The chair that Val had observed earlier had clearly been used to smash the window, as evidenced by the glass shards visibly embedded in the wood. Because the culprit lived at this residence, anything linking him to it was of no evidential value. We were looking for possible traces of blood from the deceased.

At 2:00 p.m. we drove to Tullamore Regional Hospital accompanied by Sergeant Mary Mangan. The mortuary there was a modern facility located at the rear of the property. People are often surprised to learn that our job brief included attending forensic post-mortem examinations carried out by the state pathologist, even for suspicious deaths that may not turn out to be murder. Our role was active and hands-on, assisting the state pathologist and following her direction. The objective was to photograph, document and record the post-mortem, taking possession of any samples retrieved. The photographs would then be provided to the state pathologist for reference purposes during the compilation of the post-mortem report. We would later send these documented samples for analysis to Forensic Science Ireland and the blood samples to the State Laboratory for a toxicology report, which shows whether alcohol, drugs or medications is present.

We always tried to arrive early for the post-mortem as there was some setting up to do in advance. It could look like we were bringing the full contents of our van as we arrived but all the equipment was necessary. Camera, backup camera, protective white suits, gloves, foot coverings, brown paper evidence bags for clothing, assorted long and short swabs, small plastic evidence bags and preprinted sticky labels with the deceased's details, date of birth and date of post-mortem. As obsessively compulsive as it might sound, each item was accompanied by a backup, just in case. As with taking evidence at the murder scene, there was only one chance to get it right at a state pathologist's forensic post-mortem; having a backup camera and equipment was the safer option. 'Two is one, and one is none' was again the mantra on such occasions. A little preparation and consideration for what might never occur served us well over the years.

Preparing the labels for printing was always a poignant task. Typing the deceased's name and date of birth onto the template, followed by the date of the post-mortem, gave pause for reflection.

Only hours before, the dead person lying on a trolley was alive; little could they have realised that their name was soon to be on a post-mortem label.

Despite the sombre nature of the job, meeting with the now-retired state pathologist Dr Marie Cassidy was always a pleasant experience. Her friendly and bubbly nature endeared her to all who met her and her witty down-to-earth ways were an example to all in high-profile public positions.

Mark and I told her the story of Valerie's near demise and with straight faces announced that we would not have been found wanting in carrying out our post-mortem duties had she ended up here in a different capacity. Valerie immediately knew what we were up to and was more horrified at the thoughts of us being present, camera at the ready, than her near brush with death. Standing closest to her, I received a hefty thump to the chest,

'Don't worry, Valerie, I wouldn't have let them in the door near you,' quipped Marie.

In our briefing with Marie in an adjoining office, she took notes on the deceased's background and the circumstances of the stabbing. Mark continued with his photography duties while Valerie and I took responsibility for samples and note-taking. Then it was time for me to step into the examination room.

The mortuary in Tullamore is spacious and well-equipped, with all worktops and surfaces stainless steel for hygiene purposes. Setting out our evidence bags, sealed swab containers and documentation on a vacant end worktop, I took in the outline of Akadiusz's body beside me, the familiar shape traced by the sheet which hung loosely, raised at the feet and head and wider at the shoulders: the outline of the human form. I was alone with him now.

The stillness of these solitary moments always offered me cause for reflection. As I worked silently, fixing labels to the plastic evidence bags and noting in blue marker the exhibit numbers that would identify each item of clothing until a verdict was reached at trial, I thought of the deceased and his mourning family. A cold and clinical atmosphere prevailed with the bright overhead lighting, stark white walls and dull grey silver hue of worktops, gurney and sinks. It was broken only by the injection of life and humanity when Marie and my colleagues entered later.

Mark and Valerie arrived in first, kitted like me from head to toe in white suits, foot coverings and blue latex gloves. Emmet, the mortuary technician, was followed by Marie kitted in her blue medical scrubs, the lower sleeves protected by elbow-length latex surgical gloves to best facilitate her detailed examination. She adjusted the clipboard containing her post-mortem note sheets and checked that we were all are good to go.

The early stages of the post-mortem were busiest for me on samples. When the sheet was removed from the body, I folded it carefully and placed it in a large brown evidence bag, so it would be available for forensic examination later. Likewise, the victim's tracksuit bottom, underwear, socks and footwear, as well as other items recovered at the scene, were each gently placed in brown paper evidence bags to ensure preservation of minute traces discoverable at Forensic Science Ireland. These bags were always used for clothing and material that might have bloodstain evidence on them, the breathable paper preventing mildew and mould that would ferment in a plastic bag. Marie now moved quickly, taking under-nail scraping swabs from left and right hands, hair samples and bodily swabs. The nail-scraping swabs were different to the regular ones; they looked like a stronger version of a toothpick and were used to scrape beneath the nails for potential evidence from the assailant as the victim defended himself. Each of these sealed swabs were opened and presented to Marie in the sequence required, with Valerie and myself operating a relay system to ensure minimal delay and that the open unsealed plastic evidence bag was ready to receive each correct sample.

Reprieve came when Marie walked around the body, noting every visible blemish on the skin surface. I took the opportunity to double-check that each sample was labelled and packaged properly before sealing them and later presenting them for Marie's signature. I then opened my A4 notebook in which I made a written note of each sample and the exhibit number that I had assigned it.

It was now Mark's turn. As he prepared to photograph those injuries indicated by Marie, Akadiusz's body was carefully washed and rinsed to expose all wounds, which were meticulously documented. Marie addressed every minute blemish mark or wound on the skin surface, holding a scaled rule to each, which Mark photographed accordingly, the whirr of the shutter release and the sound of the flashgun burst and its unique low electrical recharge the only interruption to the silence. How did I cope with these forensic post-mortems, knowing what was required to ascertain the cause of death? It was a combination of the detailed and meticulous attention needed to assist the pathologist and the concentration required to do the job correctly. Familiarity from attending so many forensic examinations over the years also helped. But I still always felt a slight shudder as the scalpel made that first deep Y incision into the body. Likewise the moment when the brain was delicately extracted for examination, although the continuous repeated exposure dulled any outward expression of recoil and veered it towards investigative enquiry. As the years progressed, my thoughts while standing there would drift with wonderment to the complex marvel of nature. Looking at the intricate physical structure of the brain, I would often gaze in silent contemplation, questioning how this inanimate object could once have held thoughts, feelings, fears, emotions, the very core of our conscious being, and yet now was lifeless and motionless before me on a gurney. Those invisible, unquantifiable properties no more.

Remarkably for a fatal stabbing, there was relatively little blood present on the clothing or the body. As Marie conducted her internal examination, we spoke about the circumstances of the case and the fact that after being stabbed he had walked around the corner and into the shopping centre before collapsing. The previous day's CCTV footage had suggested that multiple stab wounds would be the cause of death, but it was now evident after viewing the body that this was not the case. There was the deep defensive wound across the palm and little finger of the left hand and a small, innocuous-looking stab wound to the left of the chest. Marie found that that single stab wound had extended through his chest and into his heart: it was the fatal wound that had killed him. She explained that the deceased's heart had kept beating as he walked and, as the blood haemorrhaged through his heart muscle, there was simply no longer a sufficient supply to keep pumping.

'This poor guy was a dead man walking,' she said gently in her unique Glaswegian accent. I had often heard of the phrase being shouted aloud to death row inmates en route to their final execution, but never used in this literal sense. It made me reflect on that fine line between life and death, as I recounted the 57 steps I had paced from the stabbing location to where Akadiusz Czajkowski had collapsed. This man had walked to check himself in the toilets, unaware that his time had come. A slight change in position or a stumble and the knife could have entered his chest either side of the heart, possibly hitting a rib or the sternum; he might have survived.

There was a suggestion that the deceased had been using an alias and we set about establishing his identity by taking his fingerprints. This involved applying a small ink pad to the inside finger and then rolling the paper in a curved metal spoon-type holder to allow the pattern of the fingerprint replicate on the paper. Rigor mortis could make this an awkward process. Despite the violence I had witnessed in decades of frontline policing, the basic human default instinct not to hurt was deeply embedded, all the more so when handling a dead body. It was surreal to hold the hand of a murder victim, cold and clammy to the touch, as I manoeuvred the fingers to the optimal position. Prying Akadiusz's stiff cold fingers outward, the defensive wound revealing the internal tendons with the movement, the momentary thought that I was hurting him quickly subsided.

As I worked on the left hand and Mark took care of the right, my mind drifted back to my childhood fear of death and how since then death had become intimately familiar, not alone in thought but in physicality too. That existential anxiety had been replaced by a realisation that death was an inevitable outcome of having the privilege to live. The unlikelihood of life happening at all struck me; how for each of us it depends on thousands of random encounters throughout previous generations. Were we ultimately accidents of chance and biochemistry?

Driving home alone later that night, I contemplated a man being stabbed to death in broad daylight on a rural town thoroughfare while people went about attending to their daily business. I thought of his heart pumping for the last few times as people passed by him, shopping bags in hand, unaware that they were looking at a 'dead man walking'. I also reflected on how Valerie had survived this incident intact, selfishly considering how I would have been unable to face her family had events had turned out differently. It transpired throughout the course of the investigation that the murdered man was a drug dealer who had threatened the 25-year-old Rihards Lavickis and his family over a €100 debt, which had culminated in the chair through the window incident we had initially attended, and then the subsequent death. Rihards pleaded not guilty to murder but guilty to manslaughter. After four hours of deliberation in March 2018, the jury failed to reach a verdict and the case went to a second trial. One year later, a jury found him guilty of murder by unanimous verdict and the Latvian native was sentenced to life in prison.

I have passed the area many times since, recalling the tragic lives ruined and Valerie's stairway dance with death, and each time feel profoundly grateful for her survival. My image of Rue Noyal Chatillon was no longer the idyllic one conjured up on that fateful morning, but that of a lonely street sign wrapped in crime scene tape, the loose length fluttering and flapping in the breeze.

# CHAPTER 12

# SIG SAUER SADNESS

The shape and outline of the semi-automatic handgun gleamed with a threatening menace a few feet from my face, the rugged black exterior hiding the deadly payload stacked in the magazine. The metallic snap of the breech signalled the chaos to follow. I recoiled as the first four rounds were discharged, empty shells ejecting from the chamber as the trigger was expertly squeezed. Wisps of blue-grey vapour waft dispersed as another six rounds exited, the loud report of each shot shattering the silence.

My senses were assailed as the empty shells continued their ejection trajectory, tumbling as they hit the ground in a disjointed dance-like pattern. The smell was faint and acrid, tinged with a hint of burning. Another five shots followed in quick succession and then a final sharp metallic click as the breech locked into place, exposing the now-empty chamber benign once more. Without any spent shells to disperse it, the last strand of vapour lingered a little longer.

I remained stock still, conscious of my proximity to this compact engineered piece of deadly force and watched as the empty magazine was smoothly ejected and replaced in one fluid motion. The breech was returned and the sequence of the controlled fury of explosions began again, propelling the tiny lead rounds down the barrel at 1,250 feet per second, invisible to the naked human eye. Each bullet ripped into its target a fraction of a second before my ear registered the gunshot sound, the lethal force of each one concentrated and unleashed in a single tiny impact space. Once again, the metallic rasp of the breech locking into position signalled that the magazine was empty. The skilled shooter changed from a two-hand to a right-hand grip, his feet subtly shifting as his stance altered.

This time there was no reload. Instead, the shooter swivelled his body position and, staring at me as I returned his gaze, commanded clearly with a firm voice.

'Stand back and follow my signal.'

I mimicked his movements, carefully disguising the cascades of confusion surging through me. Here was neither the time nor place to process what I was really feeling, which was pure and unadulterated horror. This was the red zone, that forbidden area where live weapons were being fired. Slowly and deliberately, I took a couple of steps backwards, keeping my eyes on the gun, bitterly conscious of its destructive force now neutralised. Finally reaching normal range safety and removing the Peltor ear defenders, the firearms instructor holstered his Sig Sauer P226 before turning to me.

'Was that okay?'

I was there as part of the investigation into the murder of my friend and colleague Garda Colm Horkan. It was February 2022 and, in his quest to leave no stone unturned, Detective Inspector John Costello had arranged for me to meet a weapons instructor at the indoor firing range at the Garda HQ in Galway. The purpose was to have him fire an exact replica of the Sig Sauer weapon used in the homicide, as part of a re-enactment of CCTV footage retrieved from Main Street, Castlerea, from that fateful night. Mounted in a fixed position high on the wall of a local business premises and aimed downwards, the video surveillance failed to capture the murder itself, but a small segment had shown Stephen Silver firing, arm outstretched without supporting grip, and the recoil of the weapon he had forcibly taken from Colm's possession clearly visible. Having it replaying continuously in my head would have been bad enough to contend with without watching Colm's last moments playing out in cruel real-time. Detective Inspector John Costello had me record the professional marksman firing the weapon single-handedly to compare hand movements or involuntary reactions to the recoil with those evidenced on the zoomed CCTV footage. The purpose of the exercise was to firstly see what the firearms experts made of the arm movement and the fact that the gun had been fired single-handedly, with no supporting grip. John made no mention to the marksman of his own expertise as an original member of the Garda Emergency Response Unit, the elite anti-terrorist unit established to combat the threat and subsequent proliferation of armed criminality following the ceasefire in Northern Ireland, its members dedicated beyond belief and trained to the most exacting standards.

Together we reviewed the footage from the tripod-mounted camera positioned inside the red zone and did some further run-throughs with positional changes. I locked the Secure Digital card and returned to the briefing room.

Earlier in that same briefing room he had shown us the original CCTV surveillance footage from that fateful June night in 2020. The footage was in black and white and of reasonable quality, and Main Street, Castlerea, was easily recognisable, with the exterior of Glamorize Boutique clearly visible and a silver Toyota Avensis parked against the kerb on the far side of the road. The timestamp at the top right of the screen read 11:50 p.m. as the milliseconds counted furiously down, the time not accurate. My eyes focused intently, waiting for even the smallest change in the scene. Statements from the time detailed how Colm had responded to a call regarding a motorcycle being driven dangerously, with the motorcyclist performing burnouts in the Knockroe part of the town. Having patrolled that area to no avail, he had driven his unmarked black Hyundai i20 saloon detective branch car along New Road and turned right up Patrick Street before stopping at the T-junction with Main Street, where he encountered Stephen Silver. The eyewitness account of James Coyne, also present, described Colm stopping to speak with them both at the intersection and Stephen Silver leaning into the Hyundai's open window, possibly spitting at Colm who immediately got out of the car and approached him. Silver was then said to have adopted an aggressive tone and posture with Colm and struck him.

Just then, Garda Aiden Fallon and his passenger seat observer Garda Helen Gillen were passing in the Castlerea patrol car, having earlier discussed the possibility of James Coyne's involvement in the reported motorcycle burnout incident. I focused on the screen's motionless CCTV street view, the only visible activity being the relentless countdown clock in the top right-hand corner. Then, slowly, the marked patrol car passed through the frame having just, outside the captured footage range, passed the stationary detective branch Hyundai in the mouth of the junction, James Coyne standing, and the initial physical struggle between Colm and Stephen Silver. I found myself wondering whether the footage was playing at real-time speed or slower. In their statements and subsequent evidence at trial, Garda Gillen and Garda Fallon each described seeing James Coyne standing on the pathway as they approached the junction and two men 'grappling' in the doorway of Gannon Travel on Main Street. They both recounted passing by the men and then hearing gunshots as they reached some parked cars. This appeared to tally with the segment of footage that I was viewing but my mind was racing. The tape rolled on and then the footage changed to that of another CCTV camera recording the view back up the street towards the junction, but from the opposite side of the street. I could see the patrol car coming to a stop and then turning across the roadway. The two gardaí exited the patrol car on foot, and walked slowly and bravely towards where Stephen Silver was still holding the gun. Colm had just been shot 11 times, further up the street and out of the range of the CCTV camera.

Garda Helen Gillen described hearing a metallic scraping sound as the gun impacted the road surface when Silver threw it away, while Garda Aidan Fallon checked on Colm's now lifeless body and started CPR. It was already too late. Eyewitness accounts reported that Silver subsequently knelt, in a repeat of our encounter with him and his samurai sword, years earlier.

I asked Detective Inspector John Costello to replay the tape. While the others concentrated on the gunfire segment, I was fixated on the patrol car, the clock countdown and the tape speed. Once again, I watched intently as the patrol car slowly entered and passed through the frame, playing out in my head the sequence as it must have happened, just out of CCTV range. I knew intimately the clear view while approaching the junction from the Tully's Hotel side, having driven along that street many thousands of times both in marked patrol cars and the CSI van. I watched as the CCTV angle changed to show an outstretched hand holding something as it moved upwards. We now knew from the zoomed footage that it was the gun in his hand with the firing action visible. The footage didn't capture Colm, James Coyne or Silver, just his extended arm firing.

While the others were making their way to the briefing room, I returned to the red zone to retrieve the tripod, where I paused for a moment to take in my surroundings. The walls were heavily padded with a thick black foam-like material, all sound from the outside world was excluded, and I was alone, my mind racing after what I had just viewed. I picked up one of the ejected shells lying scattered on the ground, which had cooled rapidly from its firing temperature of 300°C. Looking at the small indentation made by the firing pin contact, I rotated it between forefinger and thumb and contemplated the empty cylinder, just darkness. Flinging it with all my power against the padded wall, it silently rebounded from the spongy surface, clinking as it hit another shell on the floor. As I flicked it away with the toe of my boot, a deep sadness rose slowly through my body and passed the rear of my throat. Colm's death was as raw as if it had happened only yesterday. Viewing the footage had been difficult to absorb. Returning to the office, I backed up the camera footage from the Secure Digital card and filed it away, hoping that in some small way it would help Detective Inspector John Costello with his reconstruction in preparation for the approaching Central Criminal Court Trial.

That evening my family gave me a wide berth, knowing something was up but that I would not discuss anything work related. I couldn't stop the footage playing over and over again in my mind, alongside the sequence of events that were not captured and ended up going to bed still preoccupied with it. Eventually I drifted off into a half-sleep and then slowly into a deeper one, in which I had a vivid dream about Stephen Silver. He was in front of me, samurai sword in hand, and he was threatening me. I was back in the room where the original samurai sword stand-off occurred. I positioned my hand to guide him towards the door, but suddenly he struck out and connected with the palm of his hand to my neck. As I stumbled backwards, he immediately followed up with a martial arts kick and the oxygen was sucked violently from my lungs as I doubled over, winded and unable to breathe. Instinctively, I reached out to grab him in an effort to protect myself, but it was futile, he was too strong. Looking up, I saw the frozen look in his eyes and could not understand. The location had changed. I saw Gannon Travel and the black Hyundai detective car at the junction, window open, engine running, lights on. 'Where was Colm?' I wondered. Silver and I now struggled, with me clinging to him like a boxer desperate to stay standing. I sensed a car approaching and welcomed the familiar white fluorescent-striped patrol vehicle. It kept going, however, and now I was rolling on the road and Silver kicked me repeatedly.

I saw James Coyne's distinctive shaved head and tattooed neck standing at the junction corner beside Colm's Hyundai detective branch car with a strange look of fear on his face and wondered why. Time slowed down and I now understood: there was a handgun in Steven Silver's right hand, and he struck me across the forehead with it and then pointed it down at me. First, I felt the searing heat in my shoulder and then the instant gunshot. More gunshots, more heat, neck, shoulder, back, arm, thigh, stomach, chest, hip. Time shuddered to a pause, and everything was in extended slow motion as I drifted gently upwards. I was overhead now, looking down on the street below as the gun arced slowly through the air before bouncing across the road surface. There was no sound. Steven Silver was kneeling, James Coyne was running, and two gardaí were cautiously approaching. One leaned over the figure on the ground, and I also looked closer to identify the face. It was mine and I was dead.

I woke with a start and sat up in the bed, drenched with sweat and breathing heavily. I felt haunted with a potent mixture of existential relief and survivor's guilt. Why Colm and not me? Same assailant, similar deadly weapons, different outcome and I wasn't there to help him.

It was no use, I couldn't sleep. I got up and drove to Castlerea, it was 4:30 a.m. My mind couldn't rest until I viewed the setting again in light of the CCTV footage, and I had plenty of time before I was due to start work. The streets were deserted and the external lighting bright as I parked my car near the T-junction and sat for a while, absorbing my surroundings, taking in Gannon Travel, New Design and further down the street, in the direction of the garda station.

I walked back slowly towards Tully's Hotel, standing in the middle of the empty road at the place where the driver of the patrol car would have been that fateful night. Walking towards the junction so familiar to me, the vista opened up and I had full and clear visibility through it in the Ballyhaunis direction. The silver

Toyota Avensis visible in the CCTV footage that night was still parked in the same position as before, further down the street on the far side of the junction. Crossing the street to stand in the exact spot where Colm had died, I silently recited a little prayer for his soul. With the approaching sound of a milk van doing its rounds, I moved onto the footpath and returned to my car for a long-handled metre measure tape. Placing the wheel on the ground, I reset the counter and stepped out the distance from where the junction view opened up to where the patrol car eventually stopped. Seventy-seven metres. Then, standing motionless with my back to the Gannon Travel doorway, I looked at the damaged plasterwork high on the plinth over the building opposite, where a bullet had struck and the sadness for Colm's loss once again gripped me.

A small fox appeared from behind a bin at the side of the bank carpark across the street. It was heading straight towards where I stood. Making eye contact, he stopped and stared, his instincts alerted. I stood motionless as he decided on his next move. Establishing I was no threat, he trotted across the street and down the alleyway beside Tully's Pharmacy. I stared along Main Street, my focus vague but mind alert, taking in where Colm took his final breath. The earlier strange mash-up of dream and reality still permeated my mind as I thought about James Coyne present as Colm was murdered. Physically, he was the strongest man I ever encountered; I had arrested him for his own welfare many years beforehand on that very same spot. It was scarcely believable that I had previously arrested both Silver and James Coyne.

As I stood there deep in reflection I thought of Mark as he carried out his CSI duties, the harrowing sights as he lifted Colm's lifeless hands to check for forensic evidence. This was the harsh reality of crime scene investigation, a dear friend and colleague shot dead, the natural human emotions to be quickly suppressed, the crucial early duties at a murder scene taking precedence.

I was interrupted by the sound of an approaching car. At this stage I had reflected enough and had one more thing to do. It was now getting close to 7:00 a.m. and that magical stillness of early morning had left the air as traffic was starting to stir. I sat back into my car and came to a stop outside Tully's Hotel, looking down the street at the fateful T- junction and hoping to see a car stop exactly where Colm's black Hyundai detective branch car had been. Securing my phone on its dashboard holder, I set it to video mode and waited patiently as it recorded. Eventually a car approached the T-junction, the driver looking right and remained stationary. He paused, unsure whether I was moving or not, while I drove forward, the phone recording the clear view of the roadway and junction. The car in the mouth of the junction was perfectly visible in the exact location that Colm's black Hyundai had been, and where James Coyne had stood. I passed the door of Gannon Travel where the two men were seen 'grappling', and I continued onwards past to where the silver Toyota Avensis was parked just as it was on that fateful night. Pulling in outside Tully's Pharmacy, I replayed the video recording frame by frame before turning the car around and driving away, Main Street and the junction fading in my rearview mirror, the questions which had been rampaging in my head finally answered. I thought of my first handshake with Colm Horkan as I passed Castlerea Garda Station on the left, the black marble memorial plaque to John

Morley and Henry Byrne bathed in the early rays of morning sunlight, his name now forever associated with theirs. I looked away and kept driving.

◆

In November 2022, during Silver's first trial for the capital murder of Detective Garda Colm Horkan, Professor Harry Kennedy, consultant forensic psychiatrist, executive clinical director at the National Forensic Mental Health Service, Central Mental Hospital, Dundrum and clinical professor of forensic psychiatry at Trinity College Dublin, gave evidence of my 2006 encounter with Stephen Silver and the samurai sword. He disagreed that Stephen Silver's responsibility for the shooting was diminished because of a relapse of bipolar disorder, saying that his earlier ability to display seriously threatening behaviour with a 'high probability of causing harm' demonstrated that he was familiar with enacting a personal drama involving confrontation with gardaí. He had asserted his control and 'mastery of the situation' and then became compliant to bring an end to the confrontation.

I hadn't considered our stand-off in this way, but it was true that for an extended period that evening he had indeed held all the aces. Clad in protective boots, motorcycle leather, closed-visor crash helmet while yielding a samurai sword in an aggressive and threatening manner against two unarmed gardaí in pale-blue uniform shirts, light summer-issue trousers and light rubber-soled shoes could have been said to bestow a certain element of control.

Fourteen years later, in the cruellest, violent and most tragic way possible, he displayed 'mastery of the situation' over the ultimate choice of life or death by brutally murdering Colm. Was the samurai sword incident a trial run at drawing gardaí to an armed confrontation that he badly needed to enact?

Deep sadness still gnaws at my insides with a rasping edge, a profound melancholy about that terrible incident I cannot shake off. Many times I have interrogated it from every possible angle, before smothering it back down. I visualise it travelling along my core, connecting my viscera with the neural networks that trigger the subconscious of my brain. It forms in exact sequence, playing out with what I have viewed and carefully considered.

The State refused Silver's guilty plea to manslaughter by reason of diminished responsibility. On 17 November 2022, the Central Criminal Court jury failed, after three days of evidence and nine hours of deliberation, to reach a verdict and a retrial was ordered.

At Silver's second trial on 15 March 2023, he changed all the barristers representing him. The jury deliberated for a total of 8 hours and 39 minutes before returning their unanimous verdict that he was indeed guilty of the capital murder of a garda acting in the course of his duty. The following month he was jailed for life with a minimum time to be served of 40 years.

After the conviction, I needed to visit Colm's grave again and consider things in his presence. A call to his father, Marty, was long overdue. The samurai sword had remained for the longest of times on the top shelf in the sergeant's office, benignly lying there gathering dust, a reminder of how fate can play out so cruelly in different ways, with me and my colleagues retired, alive, healthy and well, while Colm lies lifeless in his final resting place.

# CHAPTER 13

# DEATH IS NEAR, NOT FAR

t was Halloween 2023, and an evolved relic of ancient customs, rituals and festivities was playing out before me in the form of small children calling door-to-door in their fancy dress, now and then throwing careful glances back at their parents and other carers, some of whom were also bedecked in costume. The miniature 'walking dead' wandered joyously with buckets in hand even as they compared their accumulated bounties with one another.

Every now and then, my eyes were drawn to the plume of firework trails in the distance, which briefly lit up the sky in a suburb where such innocence was only too often absent. There, malice had frequently propagated to inflict terror on those who quietly resided behind drawn curtains and shuttered windows.

Driving out of Dublin, through these streets I had policed, I wondered to what extent the licence to vandalise and destroy had escalated in the intervening 30 years since I had first witnessed it through inexperienced eyes. I recalled gaping in disbelief as ambulances and fire engines were stoned and attacked by baying mobs of feral youth while emergency crews responded, merely trying to do their duty. Cars, wheelie bins and anything plunderable in the vicinity were seized, stolen and presented as an infernal sacrifice … to what unknown deity? Patrol cars were stoned many times throughout the year, their seasoned crews no stranger to the Halloween spectacle of mayhem repeated across this city suburb as if a necessary ritual on this night of ancient lore.

I was drawn back to memories of Halloween in my own youth and the innocence of early school years, ducking in basins of water with a few ten pence coins at the bottom or igniting homemade key- or bolt-bangers with an explosive sound, often rupturing while going out in a literal blaze of glory.

I had no idea where these customs of deliberate vandalism had originated from. Maybe they descended from the frights and noises of ancient ritual, before being adapted much later into the American trick-or-treat that evolved from our Samhain festival traditions during the mass emigration of the 1800s, only to return to Ireland modified and commercialised in more recent decades.

As I exited the M50 and took the N4 my mind was in reflective mode. A few weeks beforehand I had visited the National Museum and sought out the priceless gold lunula and discs of the Coggalbeg Horde. As I stood there, I felt a quiet satisfaction at the role that my crime scene investigation had played in their recovery and now prominent placing. For the ancients that crafted those stunning artefacts, winter came with the existential fear that times of abundant light and bounty might never return. Ruled by such patterns of darkness and light, seasons of plenty and scarcity, warm summer comforts and damp winter hardships, they paid close attention to the rhythm of things. Captivated by the eternal mysteries of life and death, their rituals, offerings and extravagant memorials were propitiated to ensure that the full force of the sun would indeed return to bring the anticipated daylight, the renewed year and the seasonal rebirth.

Samhain itself dates back 2,000 years, when the belief was that spirits and ghosts visited us during the darker half of the year when the veil of separation between this world of the living and the otherworld of the dead was at its thinnest.

In the country's much-feared misty and ethereal bogland areas, returning spirits were kept at bay through ritual presentations or deposits to win their favour. There was an annual tradition of lighting large bonfires to illuminate and protect those leaving the offerings of food and possessions, disguising themselves so they wouldn't be recognised by harmful spirits; this is the origin of the masked costumes of today.

Yet long before Samhain, pre-Celtic communities had demonstrated an intellectual capacity and intuitive awareness of their own with regards to this season of change, decay and darkness. On a par with ancient Egyptian, Aztec and Sumerian civilisations, our forebearers applied great architectural complexity and ingenuity to construct magnificent burial chambers of their own on a bend in the River Boyne, County Meath. Two weeks later, I finished an early morning talk with the Leaving Certificate students at St Patricks College, Navan and afterwards took a short drive.

It was a stunning morning with clear blue skies and the sun slowly eased the frosty nip in the air. I stood in turn in front of megalithic Newgrange, the breathtaking views back across Brú na Bóinne, the Boyne Valley, County Meath, easily affirming the strategic selection of this location. The massive entrance stone with its unique tri-spiral carving welcomed the gathering group as we prepared to enter the interior. I paused briefly to savour this step back in time, replicating the ancient ceremonial journey and pilgrimage to another world. The pebbled stone pathway crunched underfoot as I squeezed down the narrow passage. It was stunning.

As I edged forward, my hands trailed along smooth slabs of stone, fingers tracing the intricate lines and spirals which a skilled stonemason had once carved.

Both the 60-foot-long passageway and the inner burial chamber were lit up, revealing the knowledge and craftmanship which had kept the vaulted pyramid roof stone slabs in place for the past five millennia. Ninety-seven massive kerbstones sat overhead without cement, mortar or pinning; their leaning inverted mass suspended. There was no feeling of danger or risk of collapse, just awe at their magnificence. It was remarkable to stand in this place and see that it remained dry, with no sign of water ingress or even a trace of dampness, an extraordinary feat considering the time span elapsed and the oceanic volumes of rain that had since soaked the millennia.

The tour guide turned off the lights to provide a feeling for the winter solstice due in just over a month's time. At sunrise on the shortest days of the year around the winter solstice, 21 December, the burial chamber is naturally illuminated over a period of approximately 17 minutes by a narrow beam of light which penetrates the roof box and reaches the floor of the chamber, gradually extending to the rear of the passage. As the sun rises higher, the beam widens within the chamber so that the whole room becomes dramatically lit up.

A hushed silence fell on the group, and I crouched on my haunches, eyes adjusting to the darkness. Looking back down the lower entrance passage, a narrow shaft of light became visible after a few seconds and bisected the darkness in an elongated triangle of pale illumination. Its peak stopped short of the chamber but offered just enough faint brightness to make out with the benefit of artificial lighting a portion of the interior with its ancient inscriptions. I thought of the lives of the five human remains discovered here during an excavation and wondered about the success or otherwise of their particular journey to the afterlife.

Yet the consistent allure of Halloween potentially still represented that part of our collective memory fascinated by death and the possibility of an afterlife. In all our technological advances, might we too still be seduced by the fantasy that our daily rotation around the axis, which provides light after darkness and a new dawn after the spent day, would somehow continue endlessly for us? Were we, in this scientific era, equally and in our own way seeking alternative distractions from the urgency and preciousness of living in a present moment beyond the tensions of opposites?

Some of my favourite days are those mellow with autumnal beauty, still-mirrored waters, golden hues and russet shades. As October advanced into November this was the season of natural decay and the onset of winter, the darkest night drawing ever closer. That we too would face our own winter was an inescapable fact. It was something I had cause to reflect upon deeply over the years, as I tried to resolve my childhood fear of death while dealing with my prolonged exposure to death – in its sudden, violent and murderous manifestations – over a 32-year career. I was more conscious than ever of the brevity and beauty of this fragile human existence.

It was November 2023 and I had been up since 5:00 a.m. working on these pages. Although winter as per calendar, dawn revealed itself in an autumnal glory, and I walked to the patio door to absorb the view. Golden, brown and yellow leaves glistened in the haze with just the barest outline of the sun breaking through. Silver cobwebs dangled with delicate dew droplets on an evergreen bush's surface while the lawns shimmered with a blanket of mist suspended mid-air, not a puff of a breeze to be found. The scene was breathtaking in its simplicity and stillness and, gazing at it, I found myself reciting aloud, 'Season of mists and mellow fruitfulness, / Close bosom-friend of the maturing sun'.

Absentmindedly, I turned to the bookshelf and scanned the spines of the books it held. *Poems For Life* was among them, and when I took it out discovered a bookmark on the page containing John Keats's famous verse, 'To Autumn', which commences with those very lines I had just invoked. Had some old memory been disturbed, of this poem being here in this book or was it just serendipity? If so, I did not remember. Given my strong ability to recall details, it didn't seem likely.

My son Paul was just as bemused as I was when I asked him about it, saying that his bookmark had most likely been placed there at random; he didn't know why it had been positioned at Keats's poem.

I certainly had no difficulty recalling how, a few years back, I wrote inside my copy of Seneca's *On the Shortness of Life* a list of the years since my birth, arrogant enough to have awarded myself an expiry date of 2055. Drawing a line through each year as it passed, never to be experienced again, I was starkly reminded that I had already lived more of the years I had given myself than I had left (assuming my expiry date is correct). Such hubris. In my bones I knew death could happen at any moment and I needed to be ready, so that when it came, I would harbour no regrets.

Having frequently contemplated my mortality over the years, I was still no closer to penetrating its secrets. But it wasn't until I began experiencing health problems that I began to understand these words of Confucius: 'We all have two lives, and the second begins when we realise we only have one.' While the dead had appeared frequently to me in strange dreams, replaying of some of the lifelong exposures I had been through, there had never been any messages from, or even hints about, what might await me on 'the far side'.

This raised the logical question as to whether life on this blue and green planet floating alone in the vast empty void of space might be as good as it got. The sheer unlikelihood of our very existence also troubled me, with the probability of sustainable life surviving on this lonely floating speck of dust orbiting one inconsequential star out of billions of others supposedly defying odds in the region of 1 in $10^{2,685,000}$ (one in ten to the power of two million, six hundred and eighty-five thousand).

Moreover, the exact mathematical sequencing of random events which needed to occur in the specific order and linear structure back through the chance encounters of every generation of our predeceasing parentage to the commencement of human life was itself mind blowing. Not to mention the narrow odds of every single personal ancestor from Homo sapiens back to the very origins of existence living to reproductive age. Did being here and now really represent an unbroken lineage going back four billion years? Or was there something else I hadn't considered?

◆

Back in 2001, on arrival at a camping holiday in France, I had taken our then four-year-old son to the pool complex, a large oval-type configuration. My swimming skills were weak, and Paul was wearing water wings for buoyancy. Floating contentedly but cautiously, he used the pool's edge to propel himself alongside to where I was standing at what I thought was a safe depth. I reassured him as he proceeded and built his confidence by towing him a little further out from the side, supervising as he paddled around.

Belatedly, I realised that I had stepped back over an unseen ledge to the deep section of the pool. The pool was configured in an L shape, and I was unaware there was no separation between the shallows and the depths. Suddenly I disappeared from view, clawing and grasping with nothing to hold onto, dropping backwards like a stone without buoyancy and swallowing water. My disoriented brain struggled to process that I was sinking fast with my feet now above me. Panic hit as I realised Paul was in danger, alone and unsupervised as I plummeted. Opening my eyes I made out a dark outline, a dark navy swathe of tiled surface delineating the deeper side from the regular sky-blue flooring of the shallow part of the pool.

Suddenly I was nine years of age once more, the weakest performer in our swimming lesson group. It was lesson seven and time for the deep end. I was too frightened to jump in, but the instructor's shove plunged me into the water regardless, leaving me to sink with a mixture of shock and betrayal before hitting the bottom and pushing off to the surface, where he fished me out with a long metal extension bar and plastic hoop.

But right here, right now, there was neither instructor nor lifeguard to save me. At last, feeling the bottom and reorienting by touch, my lungs shipping water and only seconds from drowning, I instinctually let my body realign, bent my legs and summoned the last of my failing strength to extend them fully and launch myself off the tiled bottom. Surging upwards, my body finally broke the surface and I flailed to grab onto the side.

Paul was laughing uproariously, thinking that this was a new comical variation of our towing game. I said a silent prayer as I pulled myself partially out of that pool, heaving, spluttering and regurgitating water from my airways, the bronzed sunbathers watching on impassively at the beached mass of pale Irish skin.

Upon recovery, I studied the pool and its deadly design, with a sheer and sudden drop from 3 to 12 feet without warning or gradual descent. I was a weak swimmer, but I suspect the design with the sheer drop might also have caught many better swimmers by surprise. Luck and good fortune had saved me, but how many times before and after had there been accounts of first-day holiday drownings? I had somehow escaped but where was my sense of gratitude and appreciation for the continued gift of life? Truth to tell, it faded quickly into the frenzied daily existence of work and raising a young family.

The term near death experience (NDE) is often used to describe those phenomena experienced by people who almost die but survive due to resuscitation or medical intervention. The common range of sensations described include a feeling of levitation or floating, the celestial sensation of a light glow appearing through distant darkness, and feelings of warmth and serenity. Accounts such as these have also been given by those who come close to death and survive without medical intervention. I had not experienced any of these sensations during my near-drowning, but another, different encounter with my mortality was awaiting me.

It was 2004 and I was alone driving the family people carrier by night on a rural roadway. I was in a hurry. Still, it was a low-octane, low-risk environment and I was driving textbook style, and, in driving school parlance, making progress.

Years beforehand I had successfully passed the month-long garda driving course, a rigorous systems-oriented approach to defensive driving techniques and a fantastic preparation for observation and safe, confident driving. Following that, I had driven without blemish the highest-powered vehicles on issue for VIP, ministerial and high-security risk prison escorts over two separate six-month stints in the transport details section based at Garda Headquarters.

While still working in Dublin, I had managed nine years accident-free in a high-octane, high-risk environment, negotiating countless emergency manoeuvres en route to life-or-death situations where response time was crucial, often narrowly avoiding being rammed by stolen cars. This was with blue lights and sirens activated, adrenaline flowing, focus, vision and concentration narrowed to the extraordinarily difficult task of high-speed response or pursuit through the unpredictable minefield of road users responding to the unfolding emergency. My garda driving instructor, Mick Delaney, had been relentless with his pre-departure checklist routines. 'Check car exterior, check tyre pressure and tyres, check oil, water and brake fluid levels. Check cabin for all unsecured items, set and adjust mirrors, set heating and ventilation. Secure safety belt.

Ignition, mirror, clutch, gear, mirror, move off smoothly. Perform a running brake test, essential when chopping and changing vehicles and drivers of patrol cars, 4x4s and vans.'

My mind subconsciously listed off the procedure drilled into us when behind the wheel on the driving course. The idea was that if all aspects were adhered to then the likelihood of an accident was greatly reduced. 'Hands safely positioned in the ten to two position, reading the road well, identifying approaching hazards as they pass. Road governed by a continuous white line. No oncoming traffic. Rough road surface with a good degree of tyre adhesion. Check rearview mirror. Clear. Safely able to stop in the distance I can see to be clear. No approaching traffic. Clear. Possible hazards to the left, farm entrance and residential dwellings. Clear. Sharp right-hand bend approaching ahead. Apply brakes to reduce speed.'

Mick would have been horrified at what happened next on that night in 2004. I applied the brakes, but nothing happened. I slammed on the hydraulics but once again there was no response. Something was jammed behind the brake pedal. Time slowed to a freeze-frame advance as I approached a sharp bend. A people carrier has a higher centre of gravity than other cars; attempting to negotiate the oncoming bend would risk turning it over.

I was heading straight at a long gravel run-off with a raised stone flower bed – quickly, I dropped the steering a fraction before feeling the car fishtail slightly. Counter-adjusting to correct, I narrowly missed the stone structure. As the car swayed back into line, continuing straight ahead at high velocity, I was in a heightened state of awareness. Everything proceeded with absolute clarity as a concrete wall, pillar and gate approached at speed. Yet again I dropped the steering and, in slow graphic motion, death approached from the front and the rear. Instinctively I lifted my hands and feet and felt the full force of the brutal impact, a huge explosion-like noise erupting around me. The car front crumpled against the massive pillar and buckled like a metallic concertina – it towards me and me towards it.

The footwell rose and crushed the pedals and floor upwards where my feet had just been, the front driver's side wheel, shock and suspension rammed back into the rapidly vacating space. The roof, steering column, wing pillar and door enveloped back towards me. A split second more had elapsed and now the onslaught from the rear was unleashed.

An unsecured drill battery flew forward at the travelling speed of the car and grazed my temple as it passed by before smashing into bits against the console. A framed picture launched over the passenger headrest and disintegrated, a corner impaling itself in the now shattered windscreen. I felt the full force of physics as my body was rammed towards the steering wheel. Luckily, the safety belt held. My left shoulder lurched violently forward, and I had a passing-out sensation as my head snapped suddenly backwards and again forwards as the weighted cargo from behind slammed into my seat and headrest.

After what seemed like an eternity, I opened my eyes but couldn't see anything and all I could hear was the faintest of hissing sounds, distant but strangely reassuring. As my eyes started to focus, I could see that I was surrounded by millions of faint white minuscule droplets, mist-like yet different, seemingly dry, parched. The particles rotated and moved, backlit, as if in a choreographed dance and I saw the faintest trace of a green glow beyond. My brain couldn't process or place the context, mysterious, ethereal, celestial, otherworldly. 'Am I dead?' I wondered to myself as a scent started to tickle at my nostrils which smelled suspiciously like gunpowder. 'Surely there couldn't be guns in the afterlife?'

My head throbbed violently and as I sneezed to release the pressure, the celestial source of the green light revealed itself to be the dashboard light glow and the dry mist the airbag powder. There was still a ringing noise in my ears but, dreading the potential risk to my spine, I was immensely relieved to be able to feel and move my hands and feet without difficulty. My neck and left shoulder ached, and I felt blood running down the side of my face in rivulets. Closing my eyes to take a deep breath, I attempted to move but was prevented from doing so by being jammed in position; the seat was pushed forward, keeping the seat belt fully taut and the release mechanism immobilised.

Reaching into my cargo pants leg pocket I retrieved a Stanley knife which I had been using earlier in the day and, cutting through the safety belt in one fell swoop, I was free. My driver's door was jammed shut from the impact of the collision, so I edged my way across the passenger seat, managed to get that door open and crawled out battered, bruised, sore and aching, my head and neck throbbing and unbelievably still alive.

Inspecting the wreckage the following day, I was stunned to see how the front driver's side had been completely destroyed by the impact, the chassis warped, and the rear of the car bent into an elevated shape. I climbed in to investigate what had caused the brake pedal to jam and soon discovered the bent outline of a small

Maglite torch which had rolled across the footwell. Stupid, careless, negligent and in flagrant breach of every proper driving skill I had learned the many years of high-end professional driving, I had nearly brought about my own demise.

Yet for all that, once again I jumped back onto life's treadmill, momentarily grateful for the reprieve and well aware that it could have been a completely different narrative on that October night, the season of decay, of death in nature, if not, on this occasion, of mine.

Some time later, I attended the scene of a fatal road traffic collision. A small van had hit a ditch and was sitting at the edge of a field, having apparently sustained minimal impact and damage compared with mine, yet tragically the driver had not survived. Investigating the scene closely, I discovered a reasonable impact mark on the ditch where a hidden stone wall had dislodged with heavy damage to the undercarriage of the van.

Looking inside I could see the telltale signs immediately, the large wound on the back of the driver's head and an assortment of tools strewn around the front cabin and dashboard. He too had been struck by an unsecured item and, while I had escaped with a cut to the side of the head and whiplash, this poor soul was dead.

Viewing his lifeless body as I helped ease it from the van, I contemplated the fine line dividing survival and death, and a wave of gratitude and humility finally overwhelmed me. I knew not when, how, or why, but now at last I had something simple, magical and special to embrace.

Someday I would eventually cross off a year on the list of years inside the Seneca book without knowing it would be my last. But in the meantime, I would rededicate myself to the wholehearted encounter with this miracle perhaps best summarised by the emperor philosopher Marcus Aurelius (AD 121–180): 'It is not Death that we should fear, but we should surely fear never beginning to live.'

# CHAPTER 14

# NOT HOW THEY DIED, BUT HOW THEY LIVED

The country cottage was nestled in a mature garden in an idyllic setting, the trees and hedges on a still autumnal evening lending an air of tranquillity to the scene. The only hint of my necessary presence was the unmarked patrol car in the driveway.

There was nobody in the living room as I entered through the open patio double door. Inside, I observed the core tenet of any initial scene examination: do nothing more than soak in the surroundings, senses alert for anything unusual or out of place. As I stood, still overcoming the subtle feeling of intrusion, I noted the intimacy of a family life on display in the sanctuary of the home, with its photographs and mementos.

I stepped into the small adjoining kitchen, neat and well-arranged, where an assortment of vases, decorative mugs and small trinkets elevated it from the merely functional. A half slice of buttered toast sat on a plate on the countertop, a resting knife neatly mirroring the angled cut. The ticking of a wall clock marked the onward passage of time, the second hand pausing briefly on each forward motion, a slight whirring sound contrasting with the prevailing silence.

'She's through there,' said a garda, who had appeared behind me, nodding towards a door before turning to respond to his crackling radio seeking an update.

Entering the hall and looking up, I took in the staircase and landing. Stairways were a common choice from which to absorb the shock and enormity of events to come, heads often buried in hands attempting to shield the awful reality. Sometimes it was in response to yet another sudden flare-up of domestic violence, a bullying partner or spouse having again wreaked havoc and injury. On other occasions, it was a space to retreat, sit and absorb bad news which had just been delivered. Often no words needed to be expressed, the sadness merely palpable as it was now in this enclosed private space. The woman sat a few steps below the landing, leaning slightly against the banisters as if for support. Her demeanour was neutral, at a glance maybe even relaxed, although a feeling of sorrow clung to the air like an unseen mist enveloping the hallway, stairs and landing. Dressed in a navy cardigan, jeans and runners, the ashtray alongside added to the air of casual unhurriedness.

I estimated her age as late thirties and, as I slowly climbed the steps, I formulated a few words of consolation.

Careful not to overly intrude, I sat alongside her on the step. Though I was lost for words, there was no awkwardness in the silence. I was close to the core of the sadness that I experienced upon originally entering the hallway, although I now realised that much of it was my own.

Changing position slightly I sat on the next step up, and carefully lifted her dark hair. The bared neck revealed the reason for my presence: a dressing gown belt used as a ligature, leading from her neck to the top of the banister post. I took the utility tool from its holder on my belt and opened the metal knife. After doing this so many countless times before, I again pressed blade against taut material, watching as it frayed in response and yielded to the sharpness of the metal. After I had done this, I sat with her a moment longer.

Finally, letting the tool drop to the step, I gently eased her lifeless form on to the landing to the familiar position of repose, arranging her as best I could, knowing that family and friends would soon gather. Carefully, I closed each eyelid, over eyes that no longer viewed a world which must have represented anguish. Then, silently, I removed the remaining segment of material from the banister post, the sadness still permeating the space. I spoke quietly to her, just a few words, part prayer, part questioning 'Why?' and, looking down at the ashtray, I wondered about the sequence of the four partially smoked cigarettes, the long white stems bent and stubbed. A faint trace of lipstick never to be applied again marking each cigarette filter.

Did each one represent a firming of resolve? Followed by another flick of the lighter and a fading hope that somebody would appear or call to avert the outcome? Perhaps joy had been extinguished a long time beforehand, with circumstances, sadness and events coalescing towards those last moments on a stairtop, silent except for the brief exhalations of smoke and the softly repeated crush of the cigarettes.

I walked into the adjoining bedroom and looked around. On the floor beside the bedside locker lay an emptied bag of anti-depressants, tabs and tabs of unopened silver-foiled pills mixed with tablets for pain relief, from which there was evidently none. I wondered if she had been adhering to her prescription protocol leading up to her death or if she had stopped taking her medication.

The trauma of a suicide by ligature or overdose often paled in comparison to the horror of a self-inflicted end by even more violent means. At such a suicide scene, my first instinct was always to try to clean up with grabbed towels, sheets or blankets – anything to lessen the shock for a family devastated at the discovery of what had happened and the loss of their loved one, so that at least they didn't have to face any physical traces after the emergency services had left. Sometimes it was impossible though to fully eliminate those after effects and, when the discovery was made later by a family member, nothing could erase the psychological impact they suffered.

A fortnight later, pulled curtains veiled the tragedy I had been sent to assess. When I entered the living room, the gut-wrenching sounds of grief coming from the kitchen were enough to melt the most hardened of hearts. A mother had returned home to find her son's life taken by his own hand. Even though the cause and circumstances appeared obvious, my presence was needed to ensure that there had been no foul play. Crossing the threshold, I flicked the remote control to silence the loud music playing on the television in the corner, its glow casting strange shadows on the pitiful scene.

The young man sat in the armchair, his hands still cradling the discharged shotgun. There was nothing suspicious, no hint of foul play, just the desperate reality of another self-taken life. I could have just declared it a suicide and left, but morally that was never an option, not with the cries of the poor mother ringing in my ears as I performed my investigation. Even had the sounds of her grief been out of earshot, it would have made no difference as I quickly got down to work trying to make the unpresentable presentable.

The room looked relatively normal, except for the young man

sitting impassively and partially beyond recognition, a double-barrelled shotgun between his legs, the barrels aimed at his head.

Conscious that there could be another live round in the second barrel, I removed the blood-soaked weapon from the young man's final grasp, my blue latex gloves turning red with blood as I did so. Then, adjusting my position to allow for the ejection of the cartridge, I flicked the lever to break the shotgun. The forward and downward motion of both barrels released a single cartridge casing, which travelled upwards and arced to the floor, where it left a bloody mark. I recoiled instinctively from the mist of blood and matter that the cartridge had projected, the wet sensation on the side of my face sending an involuntary shiver down my spine. Composing myself, I leaned the now-safe shotgun against the wall in the broken position and retreated to the bathroom to clean off, fortunately not meeting anybody en route. Peeling off my gloves and bloodied fleece top, I washed my bloodied face repeatedly as the water ran red in the sink.

As I returned to the corpse of the young man in the living room, I was highly aware that not even the darkened room could now protect his mother from what I had seen or from what lay ahead for the survivors. Through the walls I could continue to hear her piercing cries of grief which would never go away, an expensive transfer fee of suicide to be paid in continuous instalments spanning days, weeks, months and years. Leaving the closing of his remaining eye to the undertaker, I part-prayed for and part-cursed her son. Life was cruel beyond measure to those left behind to face both the painful aftermath of loss and society's collective hesitation to engage with the specific circumstances surrounding the tragedy of suicide. Grieving families, friends and loved ones often feel even more alone and devastated than ever in the face of such avoidance and incapacity to accurately empathise, only adding to the sum total of their personal trauma and distress.

As a crime scene investigator, each suicide was always followed by another one, often within the very same shift. This could seem relentless; while suicide might not feature in my caseload for weeks, suddenly there could be three or four inside a couple of days. At times like those, I despaired at what had gone wrong with this world, especially when such suicides overlapped with fatal fires, road traffic collisions, suspicious deaths or tragic industrial accidents.

Only once did I seek out the services of the state pathologist at the scene of a suicide. The injuries were so horrific that it was hard to see how they could have been self-inflicted. At the same time, everything pointed to a suicide – the note, the back story of severe depression, the slow march of isolation and withdrawal. Everything except the shocking severity and depth of the 'ear-to-ear' knife wound exposing the windpipe. I struggled to visualise how it could have been self-inflicted and, as I viewed the body from every angle and approach, I was still too baffled to make the final call. I rang my colleague Garda Mark Lawless for a second opinion and, as I awaited his arrival, I started my investigation again from scratch.

Re-reading the note written by the now lifeless hand, I spoke once more to the person who had made the gruesome discovery, carefully disguising my analytical dissection and comparison with the verbal account already given. It still rang true. Once again,

I checked the house for any evidence of a violent struggle, but there was nothing disturbed or out of place that would activate a sixth sense of something being amiss. Again, my brain acted like a rapid computing algorithm; observing, considering and, most importantly, keeping an open mind while simultaneously running a background program of every single previous death scene encountered. Each time I looked at the horror of the wounds in front of me it was blown wide open again.

When Mark arrived, I remained silent so as not to influence his interpretation, listening as he thought aloud and soaked in the surroundings. He shared my uncertainty. Between us we had almost 50 years of combined policing exposure to every single known category of violent, traumatic and accidental death, but this one had us baffled. At the subsequent post-mortem, Professor Marie Cassidy confirmed it as suicide, having only once at the beginning of her forensic pathology career in Glasgow previously encountered such repeated self-inflicted blade wounding.

During my lifetime of frontline policing, I spoke to many who had survived attempts at taking their own lives. In many instances there had been a reluctance to share their burden with loved ones, considering it easier to engage with a stranger. Some described having a longing for a simple greeting or personal connection when they initially felt down, overcome as they were by a sense of invisibility and a yearning for basic human interaction. Others explained that the desire had been to end the pain, more so than their lives. In such a dark place, they had little comprehension of how their absence would result in their suffering being immediately transferred onto their families. This is the cruel reality of the horror of suicide. One suggestion had been that a practical therapeutic approach by those skilled in intervention could help those troubled better appreciate the impact of their intended actions. Survivors also spoke of suddenly feeling suicidal, with no long lead-in of depression or anguish, no visible signs of distress.

Hospital accident and emergency departments and garda stations are very often the first port of call for many of those who attempt suicide. Hospitalisation figures from incidences of self-harm were reported as 9,705 in 2019. But after survivors' vitals are checked and cleared, they are often released once more into society, frequently little better off for the intervention. The relocation of people to community care rather than the psychiatric hospitals of old is the order of the day and the burden appears to have been transferred by the State to charities such as The Samaritans, Pieta and Aware.

Between 1968 and 1998, a 30-year period euphemistically known as the Troubles, approximately 3,700 conflict-related deaths were recorded on the island of Ireland. This eventually gave rise to peace commissions, truth and reconciliation forums, judicial enquiries, tribunals of enquiry and countless books, documentaries and articles. Official figures, across both jurisdictions on the island of Ireland, recorded that during my 32 years of frontline policing there were in the region of 24,000 deaths by suicide. 500 or so annual road fatalities were deemed unacceptable by the Irish general public, and significant resources were allocated to the establishment of the Road Safety Authority for education, training and intervention, which resulted in a significant reduction in deaths. Yet there has been no such public examination of the underlying impact caused by this tsunami of silent suffering, grief and trauma.

Actionable intervention to reduce road deaths may be easily measurable and comparatively easy to implement, compared to interventions to counteract often unseen, unknown, private turmoil. Yet this is surely no excuse for the apparent lack of assistance. Perhaps I am missing something hidden in plain view, but I do not see significant resources being allocated to address this trauma in our midst. I understand that suicide is one of the most difficult subjects to address, such is the sheer complexity and contrasting myriad of reasons for every single case. Surely, though, when suicides in Ireland are running at such shockingly high levels, we must at least try. It is only when you experience the long years of standing at scene after scene of these tragic endings that the sheer volume registers. To stand holding a beloved son, daughter or parent in your arms as a ligature is loosened, the deadweight borne, respectfully easing them to the ground, is truly a deeply moving experience. It is the deep sadness that lingers for the tragic loss of the potentially great unlived life, and the knowledge of the devastation about to be unleashed on the family that remains.

In March 2024 the Oireachtas Committee on Assisted Dying recommended the government introduce legislation allowing for assisted dying in restricted circumstances, limiting its application to those with 6 months to live in most instances, or 12 months where they are suffering from a neurodegenerative condition. I'm sure the committee balanced the complex ethical considerations in advance of making its recommendations, but I wonder are there any high level similar complex deliberations regarding the stunning volume of life lost in Ireland to suicide.

# CHAPTER 15

# BETWEEN FOUR WALLS

'Writing is thinking in public,' they say, yet personal disclosure could not be further from my nature. Privacy has been a part of my makeup for as long as I can remember, a product of my environment. The importance of staying calm, focused, pleasant, amiable and helpful to others has been deeply ingrained in me since childhood. And as one who keeps most thoughts and opinions to myself, listening to others, taking an interest in what they have to say and then acting in their benefit has served me well over a lifetime.

By 1970s standards, I grew up in relative luxury in a traditional Irish bungalow just outside the village of Lanesborough, County Longford. It was my mother Bridie's homeplace, and her mother's, and her mother's before her. My father Pat, or Packie in his native Swanlinbar, County Cavan, met my mother upon her return from Liverpool, having qualified as a nurse. They married in 1967 and soon had a family of three, sisters Michelle and Helena and me, the eldest. Ours was a childhood of kindness and care within the bounds of discipline normal to those days. My father was a uniformed garda, then detective, in nearby Roscommon.

During the Troubles in Northern Ireland, he was frequently absent. Temporary transfers to Buncrana, Dundalk, Blacklion and other border areas, often for months at a time, were par for the course. It must have been hard on my mother who had to give up work due to the marriage bar of the era and was now at home alone with three young children.

This stoicism was perhaps reflected in her later reaction to a diagnosis of pancreatic cancer. As a former nurse, she knew the outlook immediately. That she never once complained or lamented her fate was something which defined her final days. Her way was one of acceptance and gratitude that it was she who was ill, and not any of the grandchildren. There was peace in her heart, which enabled her, remarkably, to be up and about until the eve of that summer's day, 23 May 2010, when she took her final breath at the young age of 68. My father, two sisters and I were with her when she passed yet, while they grieved visibly, I stood there dry-eyed.

Throughout 20 years of policing, I had empathised deeply with countless families exposed to death's trauma and tragedy, but here I was unable to even summon a tear at the loss of my own mother. Had I become so dissociated towards death that now, at this most intimate occasion of grief, I had reduced it to matter-of-fact routine?

Standing graveside as her coffin was about to be lowered into the ground, Uncle Ciaran in the adjacent plot was very much in my mind. My eight-year-old twins, Shane and Richard, studied his headstone's inscription and, aware of the circumstances of his death, tugged on my sleeve with a question which was so important it just couldn't wait.

'Was it a single- or double-barrelled shotgun?'

'I'm not sure,' I whispered, 'we'll find out.'

I watched on, detached and without tears, pondering the innocent curiosity of these two boys kitted out a few days early in their communion best which their grandmother would never get to see, each of them holding a rose for her final resting place.

In the days and weeks following my mother's funeral, I visited her fresh grave relentlessly in a futile effort to somehow summon up the grief within, even as my crime scene investigation notebook continued to document with detachment incidents of suicide, suspicious death, murder, murder suicide and fatal road traffic collisions.

One morning, about five months later, I woke with an unfamiliar cloud of melancholy descending on me. Lying there, I realised I had been dreaming of my mother, a memory of an actual childhood event. A picnic. A rug laid out in the garden. A hot summer's day. Orange MiWadi. Now the scene shifts, and I am lying on the old brown settee in the cool of our house, my mother tenderly bandaging my knees. Both were badly cut after I tried to see how neatly they would fit into two cups. The cups broke. My knees bled. The thick blood mixed with the cup remnants and the pooling orange juice. Except that the mother at the picnic was my childhood image of her, while the mother indoors with the bandages and 1970s mercurochrome solution is how she looked just before she died.

I went downstairs to put the kettle on for a cup of tea, the fading traces of the dream still in my mind. Before knowing it, my eyes had welled up and some tears trickled down my cheeks. It was as if a switch had been flicked and a heaving sob rose up from deep within.

All that sadness which I had been incapable of accessing at my mother's deathbed and graveside now flowed. Wave after wave they came, heaving, groaning, strange sounds of keening and mourning coming from inside yet inexplicably as if from somewhere else, the despair of the world merging with my own suspended grief. Twenty minutes passed, my stomach muscles aching from the physicality of it all and my t-shirt soaking wet.

When my wife Jacqui came downstairs to investigate the sounds, I jumped up and attempted to wipe away the tears.

'What's wrong?' she asked, not making the connection.

'Ah, just a delayed reaction from my mother's funeral,' I awkwardly admitted, drying off my face with a tea towel. Incapable of being vulnerable before her, the tsunami of sadness had in any case receded, and normalcy was restored. Once more I returned to a regular workplace diet of trauma, tragedy and death, and once again assumed my default position of dutiful empathy, caring and understanding for the bereaved and their loved ones, oblivious to how some of those qualities could also have been beneficially directed towards myself.

Eleven years later, our family deathbed scene would repeat itself. This time, it was my sister Helena who was lost to cancer. She was only 47 when she died, but in another sense, I had lost her many years before. Like my mother, she was so kind, sensitive, caring, physically beautiful and intelligent. Her record Inter Certificate results were followed by similar success at the Leaving Certificate, leading her to study science at University College Dublin, her first choice. Excelling as usual in her early assignments and exams, something suddenly went wrong. Gripped by a sudden onset of anxiety that manifested in recurring debilitating panic attacks, she felt as though she was going to die. Helena dropped out of college and returned to the safety of home for respite, but even there, it was somehow to elude her.

Although she subsequently secured permanent positions with Allied Irish Banks and the local motor taxation office, something wasn't quite right, and each fell to her internal troubles. Spells of residential treatment care did little to improve things for her and Helena reconciled herself to a life of withdrawal under the watchful eye of our mother, herself blinded to the implications of sheltering an adult daughter at home, incapable of facing the world. During those years I became adept at avoiding the issue of Helena's illness. I had the ability to track well in advance where a conversation might be headed and would skilfully guide the talk well away from Helena's plight.

It is often said that if you over-protect children, it leaves them unable to cope with independent life. I once heard it described in a brutal description that holds some element of truth: If you over-protect children from the horrors of the world, you, in turn, become the horrors of the world. I often wondered silently if the grief that consumed both my grandmother and mother may have had intergenerational consequences for my sister. Could killing her with kindness have hampered Helena's efforts to reintegrate into society? Might my mother's approach have been a compensation of sorts at having lost her brother Ciaran as he went out into the world?

With time there was a gradual realisation that our mother's way of coping with Helena's breakdown was through alcohol, generating a mutually enabling situation at home whereby she facilitated my sister's continued withdrawal from the world and Helena tacitly supported her continued self-medication. Following our mother's death in 2010, Helena's withdrawal continued apace, and nobody could get through to her in terms of seeking help. She was so pleasant, engaged and chatty just so long as there was no mention of her seeking help, attending a doctor or getting treated for what appeared to be a dysfunctional situation. She was living away her adult years without socially engaging with anyone else outside the home, perfectly content to never leave the house, without any desire to negotiate what she considered a cruel and unsafe world outside. Better to live protected and cloistered without having her personal privacy threatened. Remarkably, for somebody who never visited a doctor or dentist for over 20 years, she had the most beautiful set of teeth and the perfect porcelain skin, her beauty undiminished by her relatively inactive life. Her life was not what we had wanted for her and difficult as it was to face, she appeared content and happy in the seclusion she embraced.

It is often said that a failure to address a problem, situation or conflict in a household is akin to brushing a small monster under a carpet. Every day that passes without resolution, the monster grows a little until suddenly it is so big that it bursts forth and consumes the entire house. When something important has been left unaddressed, some day it will rise up in a form that presents a problem far in excess of the original issue. One dark night in November 2020 Helena became unwell and was taken to hospital where she was discovered to have stage 4 ovarian cancer. Like her mother before her, there was not so much as a complaint or quibble about the diagnosis although I suspect deep down, she may have known. Two months later, she took her final breath at home with our shrinking family unit by her deathbed. Yet again tears flowed as my father and sister expressed their grief as she passed from this world. Once more I stood detached by her side without any trace of emotion.

Throughout all this, we had ended up caring for my mother-in-law Julie, who was in the grips of dementia. Since her husband Tom's death in 2019 she had focused on me to look after her and the accompanying emotional toll on our family was enormous. In Julie's eyes I was the golden boy and I felt it was my duty to help an elderly person in their hour of need. Each morning at 7:00 a.m. I would light her fire, dispense her medication, cook her breakfast and make sure she had everything she needed. As she recovered from a hospital spell during Covid I would bring her on long walks and little spins in the car to break the monotony for her.

Even on workdays, if I was passing, I would check in briefly, keeping her spirits up. And every evening I would return home to diffuse the aggression she had unleashed on her own daughter throughout the day, not to mention the dementia accusations that had started – that we were stealing her jewellery and clothes, that we were starving her, or leaving her alone and abandoning her. Julie's rage and recrimination was directed at Jacqui, who struggled resiliently with the demise of her mother before her eyes and whose desolation was amplified by the fact that my bond with her mother remained, while hers was lost forever. I genuinely believed I was coping with it all, my sister's terminal illness and refusal of potentially life-saving surgery, the chaos surrounding my domestic life, and the death and destruction that was part and parcel of my own professional workload.

Since childhood I had imagined being immune from life's sorrows, a young boy with the natural inclination to escape the house, explore, spend hours wandering the fields, forests and quarries. During school holidays and weekends my friends and I would disappear for hours on end building tree houses, fishing, exploring and getting up to mischief from dawn until dusk. I lived in a world far removed from Helena, having been exposed to the harsher realities of life from a very early stage. At 12 I left home to attend boarding school at St Mel's College, Longford. A harsh environment for those of a sensitive disposition or had difficulty with fitting in, my newfound persona as a footballer who excelled in the competitive climate of the time allowed me to thrive. While my sisters were excelling academically, I was marching forward into the rough and tumble of everyday life and onwards into a similarly tough work environment. Dutifully I faced each day of the newly chaotic home life, my own unaddressed monsters hidden not under any carpet but sealed deep within. Might they too someday escape to consume me?

# CHAPTER 16

# ANATOMY OF AN INVESTIGATION

t was a stunning summer's morning at Doovilra, Silver Strand, County Mayo, my favourite place in the whole world. As William Makepeace Thackery, the famous 19th-century novelist, wrote, 'To breathe, feel and see this glorious Silver Strand is a dalliance with magic, mystery and wilderness.' Yet even his words failed to do justice to its beauty. When the sun shines and the clouds part, the ocean there takes on an exquisite turquoise hue comparable with exotic shores. My first visit as a child, over forty years ago, on a family holiday, and ever since I've been drawn back regularly by the magnetic pull of its spectacular glory, never tiring of the restorative value of a swim in the adjacent Atlantic Ocean.

At the time of this particular visit, my health had been an issue and there was no better place for renewal. To bathe in those waters while soaking in the surrounding glory of raised mountains and distant Connemara landscapes was a balm to the soul. There was a cove at the very far end of the beach with a raised, rocky outcrop nestling to the side where I regularly returned to swim. The shoreline curved in a gradual crescent shape when the tide was in, revealing a golden shimmering sandy expanse as it receded. After my morning dip I would sit on a raised smooth area of rock where I dried off and soaked in the magnificence of it all. Then I'd read for a while before turning on the phone to see what was happening elsewhere.

In that magnificent early morning sunshine in June 2020, a backlog of missed calls and messages pinged relentlessly, signalling that something was very wrong. Colm Horkan had been shot dead during the night as I slept, phone on airplane mode. I quickly rang my work colleague Mark Lawless and listened stunned as he described the horrific scenes he had attended in Castlerea, County Roscommon a few hours earlier, the harrowing duties of a CSI encapsulated in Mark's account. I was shocked to hear that Stephen Silver had taken Colm's firearm and murdered him with it. We had both spoken to Colm a few times each over the previous few days with regards to a file he was preparing for the DPP. Now, tragically, his own death would likewise be the subject of a separate dossier to that same office. We reminisced on Colm's sense of propriety and his need to have things pitch perfect in his work. He had actually been scheduled to drop off his car for a service and finish work early, and we speculated on whether it was his very sense of duty which had led him to respond to that fatal call, when he could well have been on the road home.

Switching my mobile back to airplane mode I sat in silence once more, the stunning natural beauty before my eyes making this information even harder to comprehend. I waded out into the turquoise waters, initially cool but as the body adjusted feeling warmer, and swam along the shoreline before allowing myself to float aimlessly as I absorbed the full implications of Colm's death. Inhaling deeply, I released the air from my lungs and sank effortlessly to the sandy submerged beach below, gently rising and falling with the wash overhead. As I opened my eyes, the blue sky was but a mirage-like vision above as the sun's light diffused and distorted through the water. A pink jellyfish slowly drifted across the quivering skyline while I remained submerged beneath the tranquil depths, a life still to live and Colm lying motionless on a mortuary slab. Suspended there for what felt like an age, but in reality, an indeterminate few seconds, my burning lungs were relieved when I stood up in rib-high water and gasped in some precious oxygen.

Colm's senseless murder and my sister Helena's premature passing shortly afterwards propelled an intense personal investigation into the nature of life and death. My own health issues, by this stage a year in, had given me plenty of pause for deep thought. My childhood fear of mortality, combined with 32 years of professional exposure to the fragility of human existence, had become a twin-edged sword, both a source of wonder and gratitude for this priceless life I had been gifted and the basis of a deep existential understanding that life can be suddenly taken away. It had given me enough perspective to recognise when something was trivial and not worth worrying about. It had taught me to meet each day as if it were my last and had awakened an awareness in me that we do not know how much time we have left to savour what Mary Oliver described as 'this one wild and precious life'. Even through my ongoing health issues I managed to maintain a positive outlook, my core default setting not wanting to inflict my woes on anybody else. My ongoing tendency to reflect deeply had also generated a vivid recall of countless sights no eyes should have seen, images conjured up at times from the most innocuous of connections, a pattern matching a wound, a stranger in the street resembling a murder victim, a distorted shape of a shotgun injury.

My organisational abilities, analytical skills and keen eye for precise detail made me ideally suited to the role of crime scene investigator. An added bonus when dealing with the bereaved was a gift for listening and empathy. I approached each murder, violent death, accidental death or suicide with a matter-of-fact, professional manner, prioritising the deceased's family and conducting the forensic examination as best as possible to ensure justice for the bereaved.

Death was a time for calm, rational and collected thought, not for displaying emotion or upset. After the initial shock on seeing a lifeless body, my personal coping mechanism was to set about processing the scene in a methodical and structured manner. It would have been unthinkable to ask any of my peers how they coped or dealt with such matters. My cheerful disposition and reluctance to inflict negativity on anybody else meant that it was all filed away and contained within.

My first horrific workplace exposure to a traumatic sight came in 1991 when I, as a young inexperienced garda in Dublin, was detailed to preserve a body, which had been involved in a suspicious death, that had been removed to the mortuary. My job was to ensure that there would be no unauthorised interference with the corpse until the pathologist had carried out the post-mortem, thereby eliminating potential allegations as to the cause and timing of any injuries found on the body. A prosecution's senior counsel at trial could then categorically state at the opening speech to the jury that there had been no third-party interference with the body as the gardaí had been present all along.

This is a key part of any murder investigation, whereby a log is kept of every garda performing the duty so as to ensure an unbroken sequence of garda presence is maintained, and a record maintained of same. Each statement of evidence made by the accompanying gardaí established a link from the moment the body is removed from the scene to the completion of the post-mortem examination. This ensures justice and a cast-iron certainty that leaves no room for the defence to cast doubt on proceedings.

In reality, it also often meant an eight-hour tour of duty at the mortuary.

Reflecting now, I recall being somewhat apprehensive as I approached the morgue where I would be spending the night. The colleague I was relieving guided me through the body's identification formalities, which did not require a close-up inspection of the corpse. Noticing with surprise that I had brought along no food, reading material or distractions of any other sort to help pass the long night, he handed me a battered-looking copy of the *Evening Herald*. I positioned myself outside the morgue door, the only access point along the short hallway leading to a corridor that connected to the hospital complex. In doing so, I comforted myself that I was better off preventing unauthorised interference there than from beside the body.

I passed a very limited amount of time with the *Evening Herald*, beyond which each minute seemed to last an hour on that corridor. Different hues of green led down to a shiny linoleum-style floor which joined the wall with a curve rather than a skirting board. The link corridor was lit with malfunctioning double fluorescent strip lighting, a low constant buzzing noise signalling a faulty starter switch. Every so often the light would flicker and then go out, eerily leaving an inch or so glowing at the end of each tube while plunging the area it covered into deep shadow. The corpse inside the door, the shadowy corridor, the buzzing noise and seven hours still to endure were beginning to play on my young and inexperienced mind.

An hour into my night's duty, I heard a slow and lamentful whistling as a trolley slowly entered the shadowed section and rounded the corner as though self-propelled. Then I made out the vague outline of what I hoped was a hospital attendant, hunched as he powered the trolley in my direction. The wheels squeaked in protest but, without breaking his slow stride or losing his shrill melody, he merely nodded towards the door which I dutifully swung open.

The trolley transported the human remains of an accidental housefire victim. I was relieved to see the hospital attendant making an entry in a large logbook listing each deceased person who entered the mortuary and the assigned pathologist, even if I was torn between ensuring there was no forensic interference with the body I had identified and an instinctive urge to flee. As the attendant ambled across the mortuary, I couldn't tell whether his hunched shoulders were an outcome of his continuous pushing efforts or their natural default setting. Bearing the look of a man who had seen better days, still slightly crouched as if his exertions had locked him in position, his complexion was pale with deep black hollowed-out eye sockets, the visage of too many night shifts. He appeared old, although was probably younger than I am now, grey wisps of longish hair swept back from his lined forehead.

'Here, I need you for a minute,' he said, indicating the far side of the stark tiled room.

With horror, I realised what he had in mind. The trolley transporting the unfortunate burn victim was parked neatly alongside a higher steel gurney of a similar size.

'I want you to grab the sheet like this,' he instructed. Taking hold of one end of a sheet wrapped around the human remains and signalling for me to do likewise with the other, the distinctive shape was now fully recognisable even to a novice like me. 'Now mind your back,' he kindly offered, as I braced myself for the lift.

A human body when raised is heavily weighted towards the head and chest, placing the greater burden on the person lifting from there, which in this case of course was going to be me. As I gathered the sheet, I noticed there was little movement as I heaved the literal deadweight, which was much heavier than I had anticipated.

'Put your back into it, son, will you?' the hospital attendant mumbled. 'Now I'm going to count to three – one, two, three,' he added somewhat impatiently.

As I lifted, mirroring the attendant's movements as we shuffled left towards the gurney, I was stunned by the sheer weight load. Struggling with the upward movement required to complete the task, I could feel the body starting to move in the assemblage of sheets and adjusted my stance to maintain my grip. The body shifted some more and, as I grappled with keeping it raised to make the switch, the underside dragged against the higher base and parted the sheets to reveal what I had least wanted to see. The close-up view of the head and upper chest section lying burned beyond recognition left me shocked and nauseous, requiring every ounce of my focus and effort not to drop the body.

'Are you alright, son?' the hospital attendant asked, the slightest hint of what passed for a grin on his face. My ashen features surely betrayed my inexperience, and I couldn't help but feel the sheets had been strategically placed to ensure exposure.

'Fine,' I lied, standing immobile as the awful reality of what I had just seen sunk in.

He shuffled around for another while before leaving as ponderously as he had arrived with a curt nod.

As I exited the mortuary to continue my lonely doorway vigil, I looked back at the somewhat surreal sight of the two bodies now side by side, the vision of the latter made even worse by the recent knowledge of what lay between those sheets.

It was an interminably long night, throughout which my mind swung between the shocking sight of the most recent victim and an unfamiliar sorrow and sadness for his family and loved ones left behind. At the end of it all, I stuffed those turbulent emotions into what felt like an invisible container somewhere deep inside my abdomen. Looking back now, it occurs to me that I subsequently lost count of all the fatal fire locations I attended as a crime scene investigator, all the times I stood in a house with a single fatality, or when two people had been lost to the horrors of a blaze, even investigating where three people had been overcome in a single room.

There was no preparation for such experiences, little understanding of their impact and, over the span of my career, no intervention from welfare services. As the years passed, incremental deposits got added to that container core that I imagined deep within. Sometimes it felt full to the brim and, as years became decades, the risk of the seal rupturing heightened, with the contents seeping out into both my professional and personal life. Still, I managed to cope with every horrendous death scene I encountered, though occasionally loneliness would descend on me, a sense of existential sadness, more often related to the trauma of the family members I had encountered. At such times I identified with the death row inmate wrongfully incarcerated in Stephen King's *The Green Mile*: 'John Coffey cried for the world, for the people, for the things that were done. He cried for the hurt, the pain, the loss. He cried for all of it.'

Although I didn't cry, I realised that I too was slowly being incarcerated, albeit in a completely different manner. Presenting a friendly and extroverted personality to the outside world, many times it was hard to process the sheer level of death I was being exposed to in my professional life. It seemed easier to just file away such ambivalences in the invisible internal container and get on with my duties, disregarding any possible emotional toll. My default response was to detach, suppress and internalise. Dissociation was required to efficiently process fatality scenes, sometimes under intense media scrutiny, and make those crucial calls as to whether the circumstances demanded that the state pathologist should be called in. The same was true of graphic post-mortem examinations and the complex process of recording and processing evidential samples. I had no fear of facing such situations; the controlled exposure to sudden, random and unexpected events had become my new normal. Every so often though, images of those deaths would resurface at the most unexpected of times. A knife might trigger a memory of a stabbing, a butcher's shop the fatal injuries witnessed, or a post-mortem attended. A violent event I had encountered might suddenly appear in a dream sequence. I accepted these experiences as a natural part and parcel of the job. Looking back now, though, I feel that it was the sadness and trauma of the families that affected me the most; it activated my naturally empathetic disposition while my ability to investigate, process and efficiently carry out my duties, no matter how harrowing, remained intact.

As with work circumstances, my personal life seemed to be going well and everything that life threw up I handled with maximum efficiency. What could go wrong? Stuff happened to other people, not me.

In *The Myth of Normal*, Dr Gabor Maté describes how 'the most obvious, ubiquitous, important realities are often the ones hardest to see and talk about.' When I least expected it, after almost thirty years of successful containment, my body lodged an objection. While I very successfully managed to cope with the multitude of horrors I had encountered during my working life, it was coping with the onset of domestic issues that took its toll on me physically. It was in 2019 that they surfaced and struck with vengeance.

I was laying patio slabs in a DIY project at the back of the house when I wrenched my left shoulder, while pulling a cement mixer up on its stand. Afterwards, a numbing sensation arose gradually in the small and ring fingers of my left hand. I put it down to the old neck injury from my near fatal crash and, like all good Irish men, ignored it. Just like I ignored the fact that I'd been constantly tired of late, despite sleeping as well as ever – as though I had lost the ability to feel rested, often ready for bed again at 11 in the morning. To the extent that I paid this *any* attention, I attributed it to the new 10-hour shifts we were working, 6 days on and then 4 days off, totalling a 60-hour week, often at gruesome death scenes.

Three months later, while sitting reading a book, pins and needles suddenly began to prickle the left side of my face, from chin to ear and ear to temple. Having been blessed all my life with good health, I at least knew enough to realise that a tweaked shoulder did not result in facial numbness, which was closer in proximity to the brain than the back. Dr Google unhelpfully suggested possible conditions ranging from multiple sclerosis to a stroke and, with my wife Jacqui away, I consulted my colleague Valerie, who made me promise to attend to it immediately. I was hesitant but like any normal person with the spectre of a possible disabling stroke, I threw a toothbrush and toiletries into an overnight bag, got into my car and drove to the Galway Clinic which I'd read was now providing an accident and emergency service. I figured that a quick once over and I'd be done. I was wrong.

Upon arrival I was admitted immediately to the hospital, the consultant Dr Khan was baffled by my good blood pressure, strong pulse and visible alertness even as the creeping numbness and pins and needles continued to spread. He kept me in for a battery of tests and over the next five days I was subjected to magnetic resonance imaging (MRI) and computed axial tomography (CAT) scans on the brain, an electrocardiogram (ECG) on the heart and every other sort of test imaginable. Each came back with clear results and a firm reassurance that I was going to live for quite a while more. Eventually, Dr Khan returned with my blood results and announced that my Vitamin B12 and Vitamin D3 levels were extremely low. Prescribing an industrial dose of both to boost me up, he discharged me after five days of prodding, poking and daily blood draws, a cannula having been inserted for the purpose.

I threw myself back into work and home life with the usual non-stop vigour, yet something just didn't feel right, something I was unable to articulate. Around July 2019, I noticed a heavy sensation in my head as if there was a clamp attached to it and whenever I turned left or right my brain seemed to be a split second behind. My balance was also slightly off. Then one evening in August, completely without warning my balance went, and the room started to rotate violently, passing my line of vision for another lap around my head, the sensation of dizziness so bad that I thought I was going to pass out. Holding onto the couch, I tried in vain to anchor myself but to no avail. The closest visual representation of what I felt is depicted in a scene from the movie *First Man*, about the Apollo 11 moon mission. In a test space flight, the Gemini mission capsule suddenly loses control and rotates rapidly. Commander Neil Armstrong, sweat flowing from his brow and face distorted, tries in vain to fire a thruster to steady it and orient himself as Earth passes by his windows in a vicious out-of-control spin too severe for his hand to reach the lever. Houston, I too had a problem, which wasn't going away anytime soon.

Eventually the rotations subsided, and I was left there pale, drawn and afraid, very afraid. What the hell had just happened? A wave of nausea then overcame me, and I was compelled to lie down in the bedroom exhausted, curtains drawn until the next morning. This awful sickening sensation continued apace at intermittent unpredictable intervals, together with a new round of medical examinations, every type of specialist being consulted in an attempt to get to the root of the problem. I was prescribed Serc and, when that didn't work, Stemitil. My general practitioner, Dr Colm Farrell, was patience personified as I turned up repeatedly throughout 2020, struggling to describe my symptoms. He reassured me that I was healthy but, evidence suggesting otherwise, continued to refer me onwards to find a resolution. One day he even gently suggested that I might have post-traumatic stress disorder (PTSD) from my gruesome workload, to which I nonchalantly declared, 'Not a chance, Colm, this stuff doesn't bother me at all, I've been dealing with it for 30 years.'

The January 2021 evening that my sister Helena died, I had the worst spell of dizziness ever, making all that had gone before feel like child's play. I had returned home after a long day negotiating her funeral arrangements when, sitting on the couch, felt that familiar tightening sensation gripping my head. Suddenly I was in orbit once more, the room spinning Apollo-like out of control, the television flashing by my eyes like brief glimpses of Earth from the swirling capsule. Again and again and again the rotations continued, with neither thrusters nor a gyroscope to counteract them. Needing to escape the heat of the open fire I pawed my way to the front door, each forced footstep trying to follow the other and, gripped by an accompanying wave of nausea, I emptied my innards onto the driveway. Draped across the bonnet of the car while letting my temperature cool down, I wondered how I was going to get through the funeral mass and deliver the eulogy without having an attack on the altar or at the burial falling into the grave in a sudden state of dizziness. Thankfully, my worst anxieties never materialised.

By now I had begun to exist in a state of continuous hypervigilance. My gait changed as my neck became stiff from a fear that any sudden motion could provoke an onslaught, my face was permanently pale and worn, and my body seemed unable to calibrate the balance required to walk without a sense of being off-kilter.

In the aftermath of attacks my profile genuinely looked worse for wear than many of the corpses I encountered. Figuring that I might just stumble on a nugget of relief or a solution from books, I read voraciously Bessel van der Kolk's *The Body Keeps The Score*, Gabor Maté's *When the Body Says No*, Matthew Walker's *Why We Sleep*, Norman Doidge's *The Brain's Way of Healing* and other such publications. Then, serendipitously, I stumbled across a newspaper profile of Sheila Barrett, a physiotherapist based in Midleton, County Cork, specialising in dizziness caused by the vestibular system, including the parts of the inner ear and brain that help control balance and eye movements. The symptoms she described in the article sounded similar to mine and prompted further tests and internal auditory meatus (IAMS) and MRI scans on my auditory canal. Yet the constant heavy-headedness, disequilibrium and dizzy spells continued without respite, and I wondered if I would ever feel normal again.

Thanks to a cancellation, I managed to get an early consultation with Sheila. The deceptively small street frontage of her practice led to a comfortable and spacious interior. Looking up from her clipboard and viewing my prematurely ageing features, Sheila asked, 'Are you an anxious person?'

'Absolutely not', I replied with the confidence of my convictions, never having been one to sit around biting my fingernails.

'Do you suffer from stress?' she probed a little further.

'Not at all', I parried.

'What exactly do you do as a garda?' she persisted.

'I work as a crime scene investigator, those fellas you see in the white suits gathering trace evidence at serious incident sites.'

Sheila raised a quizzical eyebrow before delving further. 'So you deal with murders and death on a large scale. Does that volume of exposure not affect you?'

'No, our duty at a scene is to the deceased person and their relatives and it's no use me getting upset or emotional. We just get on with it and get the job done.'

Sheila paused for a moment as she referred to her notes.

'Have you had any stress at home during the period of these dizzy spells?'

'Yes, two bereavements', I responded, telling her of the circumstances of Helena's recent death and that of my father-in-law, Tom in June 2019 and how we had ended up caring for his wife, Julie, as the cruel reality of dementia revealed itself afterwards.

Shelia explained that stress can exist unawares in a person's system and that I should try and acknowledge it if I could. She outlined that vestibular migraine had a number of threshold features, any one on their own harmless enough but when combined with four or five other factors likely to trigger an attack.

'For example, fatigue, dehydration, an unhealthy diet, sleep deprivation, a stressor, certain foods, chocolate, high MSG foods, certain lighting or prolonged exposure to computer screens are not problematic on their own, but combined in threes or fours increase the probability of activating a trigger.'

I nodded quietly as I absorbed the information, trying to figure how it applied to me.

Before I left her practice, Sheila videoed me walking and I was stunned to see my off-kilter gait and the stiff way with which I was holding my neck fearful that any sudden movement might trigger an attack. Her final words urged me to have a close think about stressors in my life over the next while and to take better care of myself.

Throughout all this uncertainty and upheaval, I retained hope that these difficult times would be temporary. 'This too shall pass', the Roman Emperor and Stoic philosopher Marcus Aurelius (121–180 AD) told himself repeatedly in *Meditations*, a series of personal writings for his own guidance and self-improvement which I had read numerous times. 'You have the power to strip away many superfluous troubles located wholly in your judgement, and to possess a large room for yourself embracing in thought the whole cosmos, to consider everlasting time, to think of the rapid change in the parts of each thing, of how short it is from birth until dissolution, and how the void before birth and that after dissolution are equally infinite.'

Instead of focusing on an afterlife or speculating as to whatever lay beyond death, I often contemplated upon that daily transition from consciousness to unconsciousness. Lying awake after recovering from yet another dizzy spell and still too nauseous to read, I would close my eyes and wait for that moment just as sleep arrived and the semblance of a dreamlike outline was beginning to take shape. I would force myself awake and replay clearly the sequence of those milliseconds as the sleep and dream state arrived, wondering whether the arrival of death was any different.

Having attended so many post-mortem examinations over the years, I had come to realise that there is no actual physical difference between the brain of a recently departed person and that of a living one. A remarkable piece of creation, complex and stunningly beautiful in its shape, symmetrical patterns and makeup, the living brain's functionality is awesome. This structure housed invisible thought, the depths of personal conscience, and the core of the human experience. If there is an essence, a soul, a spirit which could never be seen while alive, I pondered what occurred at the exact moment of death when the breath of life transitioned into the unknown void of darkness. Beyond this, my investigative mind could not advance any further than a working hypothesis that some unknown crossing-over of that dreamlike state might occur. I had long dispensed with any notion of heaven, hell or purgatory as depicted in our Christian religious framework and was happy to accept that this gift of life was indeed a magical privilege and that any hereafter might actually consist of a vast nothingness.

Try as I might to ignore them, Sheila's parting words, 'Have a think about your stressors, your life,' reverberated continuously in my head. Combing back through Maté, van der Kolk, Walker and

Doidge, I revisited those paragraphs I had highlighted with pencil at the original time of reading, gradually coming to recognise the frequent references to PTSD. But – me? I wasn't dealing with stress from my work, I argued defensively with myself, yet not quite as convincingly as before. A few weeks later, I sat down with a blank sheet of paper and started writing a list of those difficult personal issues I had been confronting of late. To my surprise, the total quickly and significantly mounted; this didn't even include any current challenging situations at work. I laughed aloud at the extent of my own delusion and denial.

In June 2021, at the Migraine Clinic, I met with Doctor Martin Ruttledge, consultant neurologist at Beaumont Hospital, who listened intently as I listed my symptoms. I described the constant heaviness in my head and how the sensation of my brain was a split second behind as I turned my head.

'How many full clear days have you had since 1 January?' Martin asked.

I pulled out the diary I had been keeping with my symptoms. 'Roughly six days when my head felt normal,' I replied.

Martin studied the MRI of my brain on his screen. 'Firstly, your brain is in excellent condition, better shape than my own,' he joked. 'I believe you are a chronic migrainer,' he continued, 'but strangely instead of the migraine pain, you get the dizziness.' He suggested I choose one of three medications used on patients with completely different primary ailments and gave me the information sheet for each. He said that it could be up to six months before any improvement could be expected and that if this didn't work, the next could be tried and so on.

Slowly but surely, the dizzy spells started to ease yet the heavy sensation in my head remained. Was the recovery due to the medication kicking in or the appearance of home help in the form of Patsy Mulvihill for my mother-in-law Julie, and her cruel affliction of dementia? Patsy immediately recognised the urgent need for relief and went over and above in her care, often kindly bringing Julie to her own home a few days a week. 'Sure, it's no wonder your head is spinning,' she would laugh as she drove off in her car with Julie.

By the end of 2021, I started to experience a few clear days each week, which gave me some hope that things were improving. I made conscious changes in my personal life, commencing a healthy eating regime, making sure to stay well hydrated each day and learning to say that magical word – no. All my life up to that point, an ability to do this was a source of great difficulty for me. Every spare opportunity I got, I spent on the beach, for hours, and in the water at Silver Strand, its turquoise waters cleansing the stress away from my cortisol-addled system. And in April 2022, I started thinking deeply about how I could best honour this second chance at life, which I had received.

Thirty-two years as a garda meant I was eligible for retirement while still a young man. On 6 October 2022, my last day as a serving member of An Garda Síochána, I presented my talk, 'Life Lessons from Dealing with Death' at TEDx Tralee, County Kerry. A scarcely believable sequence of events followed as I successfully changed career, my unique insights and lived experiences serving me so well.

Then in January 2024 my curiosity was piqued by the story of a 16-year-old boy who, having experienced his own intense fear of death as a child, had gone missing from home in unusual circumstances. Discovering that he had then launched a personal investigation and enquiry into death, words so familiar to me from policing, I instinctively took action. Now, with health restored and the knowledge that taking action can yield amazing results I made an instant decision to travel. His name was Ramana Maharshi (1879-1950) and these insights he explored intrigued me. Arising from this, I was now propelled into a fascinating personal investigation of a completely different nature, one that would expand the boundaries of my own thinking.

# CHAPTER 17

# WHO DIES?

With just a small backpack for company and nothing to declare, I cleared security and passed through customs, weaving easily through the hordes struggling with oversized suitcases. It was 23 January 2024. The sun's warmth radiated through the plate-glass window bordering the concourse and I eagerly anticipated the cool morning air outside. Until, passing through the last double doors, I realised I was already outside. There was no temperature differential, not that you would think it from the way that nonplussed military police officer leaned casually against the metal railing. It was an overpowering 32 degrees Celsius warmer than Ireland, with high humidity mixed in for good measure.

Three rows of taxis jockeyed for position as a two-man tag team piled luggage six feet high on a yellow minibus roof rack. One threw each item of luggage upwards; the second man, balancing precariously on an assortment of suitcases, bags and rucksacks, caught it just as it commenced its descent. A quick criss-cross of ratchet strapping and the lopsided load was good to go. I watched fascinated as the roofman nimbly scaled down the side and in a seamless movement swung through the sliding door, his feet never touching the ground. Before the door slid shut, the minibus was off, a belch of dark fumes the only warning signal to the passing traffic, the load somehow remaining in place. More like an introductory sequence in a movie, this was colourful reality now before my eyes. Incredible India indeed.

Chennai International Airport is located on the southwestern edge of the city formerly known as Madras, population 12 million. It seemed as if up to half of those people were currently on the road heading deeper into the southern state of Tamil Nadu. Predicting the movements of traffic and pedestrians, something I always did when travelling as a passenger was virtually impossible and yet my taxi driver Nagaraj somehow deftly negotiated all three lanes simultaneously as cars, trucks, autorickshaws, motorcycles, scooters and mopeds effortlessly swerved around a lone cow swaggering down the motorway.

Colourful old buses with open windows and rusty roof racks tilted perilously to the left, suspensions and springs worn out from the extra load of passengers clinging to each available standing space. The hard shoulder itself functioned as an auxiliary lane, the flow of which was scarily against the oncoming traffic. Suddenly, the taxi swerved as a six-wheeler tipper truck reversed without warning into our left-hand lane, a man in flip-flops simultaneously signalling the oncoming traffic to slow down with one hand and nonchalantly guiding the vehicle backwards with the other. Skilfully rounding the truck with his hand glued to the horn, Nagaraj narrowly avoided the danger but required even further evasive action as two men on a motorcycle without a helmet between them were now heading directly towards us. Transporting a 10-foot-long steel girder, one half of it taking up almost the entire inside lane, this cross between scenes out of a PlayStation game and some of the craziest stolen-car chases from my frontline policing days was an utter assault on the senses.

Eventually the scenery dissolved into a more rustic setting, with rice paddy fields dotting the landscape. The hard shoulder now featured a mode of transport over five thousand years old, a four-wheeled cart moving towards us pulled at a steady pace by two beige bullocks harnessed like stagecoach horses, their long angular horns painted bright blue, matching the wooden rim of the cart. The driver sported a shock of wild grey hair and a long beard, his ebony skin and orange robes contrasting vividly, his load of assorted crops casually laid out behind on the flatbed.

I had only recently discovered that two Indian police sub-inspectors had never been given full credit for advancing the science of fingerprints. Hem Chandra Bose and Azizul Haque of the Kolkata Fingerprint Bureau had created a method that could be quickly used to match a set of prints to a suspect. Haque had pioneered the mathematical basis while Bose perfected it through indexation and classification. On 12 June 1897, the Council of the Governor General of India had approved fingerprints to be used for criminal records.

Named after Sir Edward Henry, their supervisor and the Inspector General of Police of Bengal, the 'Henry System of Fingerprint Classification' was used in all English-speaking countries. Sir Henry would later 'tell those who asked that it was he who had come up with the classification system in a sudden flash of inspiration on a train, when he had no paper and had to resort to noting his ideas on the shirt cuff.' Upon demonstrating the system to the British government, he was appointed assistant commissioner of Scotland Yard in 1901.

It was mid-morning when Nagaraj rounded a newly constructed bypass and Arunachala materialised through the warm hazy sunshine, the holy mountain dominating the skyline for miles around. Standing sentry over the surrounding flat countryside it appeared to be composed of many hillocks, each with its own distinctive peak and separated by a band of lush green vegetation. A few puffy clouds hovered over its pinnacle without any breeze to disperse them. On its longer sloping side, the mountain was the backdrop for four large pyramid-style structures, the colossal entrance gateways to the famous Arunachaleswarar Temple.

When we reached the outskirts of Tiruvannamalai, most of the roads were barricaded. It took all Nagaraj's charm to bypass a stern-looking police sergeant manning the security barrier. That was when I learned that I had arrived on a full moon day, an auspicious monthly event when up to a million pilgrims came from all over India to walk barefoot the 14 kilometres (eight and a half miles) clockwise around the base of the holy mountain as an act of reverence or worship. According to one tradition, the hill itself is God and in its real nature is full of light.

After checking into my accommodation, I set off for nearby Ramana Ashram, a welcome retreat and sanctuary from the effervescent bustle of people, vehicles and animals crowding the streets outside. Removing my footwear at the entrance, I joined the barefoot pilgrims as we passed through large decorative mahogany double doors, which led into a stone-slabbed entrance hall, its shaded interior immediately giving off an atmosphere of peaceful reflection as people filed slowly by, while others sat around the exterior walls in various states of contemplation.

On the right of the New Hall there was a large painted sign affixed to the wall. Against a white background, royal blue hand-painted letters told the account of a young Ramana Maharshi who, in mid-July 1896 at the age of 16 and still at school, had been struck for no apparent reason by the terror of annihilation. It had not taken the form of a gradual exposure to the death of a family member or friends but hit him in the form of the words, 'I am going to die.' Instead of panicking though, he deeply pondered this strange fear which had consumed every fibre of his being and concluded that the only way he could address it was in the form of questioning himself, 'What is death, what does it mean?' Much later, he provided the description of the event that was now in front of me:

> It was about six weeks before I left Madurai for good that the great change in my life took place. It was quite sudden. I was sitting alone in a room on the first floor of my uncle's house. I seldom had any sickness, and on that day, there was nothing wrong with my health, but a sudden violent fear of death overtook me. There was nothing in my state of health to account for it and I did not try to account for it or to find out whether there was any reason for the fear. I just felt, 'I am going to die' and began thinking what to do about it. It did not occur to me to consult a doctor or my elders or friends: I felt that I had to solve the problem myself, there and then.

I continued to read, captivated by the description of this youth who challenged death with his penetrating enquiry into the source of his being.

The shock of the fear of death drove my mind inwards and I said to myself mentally, without actually framing the words: 'Now death has come, what does it mean? What is it that is dying? This body dies.' And I at once dramatised the occurrence of death. I lay with my limbs stretched out stiff as though rigor mortis had set in and imitated a corpse so as to give greater reality to the enquiry. I held my breath and kept my lips tightly closed so that no sound could escape, so that neither the word 'I' nor any other word could be uttered. 'Well then,' I said to myself, 'this body is dead. It will be carried stiff to the burning ground and there burned and reduced to ashes. But with the death of this body, am I dead?'

I paused, transfixed by these words on the wall, which starkly reflected somewhat similar investigations of my own. Lying in bed, I had often tried to visualise the exact moment of death in some inexplicable search for understanding. Although younger at the time, it had been more of a continuous pulsing undercurrent, which returned as I lay recovering from nausea and dizziness. 'How could this be?' I thought, still staring ahead, the words blurring. I was in sensory overload now, my brain a surging mass of visual imagery, the chaotic street scenes outside combining with the words dancing before my eyes. Speechless and stunned by the circumstances which had drawn me to that place, I retreated outside, still in contemplation.

Back on the streets, I was assailed once more while walking through the throngs, bicycles nonchalantly weaving their way around yellow three-wheeled autorickshaws laden with passengers. Buses, trucks, street vendors, cars, bullock carts and pedestrians all seamlessly combined in an onward motion of organised chaos. The tinny sound of small wheels rattling on the asphalt got louder as I turned to see a man with no legs perched on a three-foot square metal sheet, wheels at each corner, propelling himself along at the edge of the traffic without anyone batting an eyelid. A family zipped by on an old 350cc Honda motorcycle, the father steering, a child seated in front on the fuel tank protected by his arms, a child holding on tight behind him and then, bringing up the rear, the mother, gloriously elegant, raven hair swept back from her forehead, beautiful yellows, oranges, purples and greens combining on her sari to striking effect as she somehow balanced side-saddle, once again all without a helmet in sight.

Pausing for a gap in the flow of traffic, I watched as a fruit vendor on the other side of the road stacked fresh yellow sweet corn neatly on his cart. Suddenly a large macaque monkey materialised as if from nowhere, grabbed a sheaf and shot across the road to where I was standing, perfectly judging the traffic and calmly sitting down beside me. Sporting the coolest centre-parting atop of what looked like a healthy head of human hair he tucked into his meal, those intelligent eyes intuiting that I posed no risk to his bounty. It was time to follow his lead and go eat myself.

As evening quickly drew in, a glorious pale-yellow moon rose as if rolling along the gentle sloping gradient of Arunachala. Thousands of devotees young and old and of every shape, size and creed were in the process of walking the circuit clockwise with the sacred peak as an axis. Some carried bags on their head or shoulders, others carried children, and the pace was set by the old and frail. Nagaraj explained that many walked it and took a bus back home, usually in time to get the children ready for school the next morning. Some maintained silence, others chanted the name of their deity and even more sang devotional hymns. When questioned on the efficacy of going around Arunachala, Ramana Maharshi is reported to have said, 'For everybody it is good to make circuit of the hill. It does not even matter whether one has faith in this or not, just as fire will burn all who touch it whether they believe it or not, so the hill will do good to all those who go round it.'

I entered the torrential stream of people as it passed by the gates of Ramana Ashram, the road now closed off and traffic diverted. As far as the eye could see there was a bobbing mass of humanity, almost all of whom were barefoot. I felt a little ashamed of the sandals between my feet and the roadway. I must have stood out – tall, grey-haired and with pale skin. I drew lingering looks and then felt the gentle touch of hands on my back and arms as people passed. What struck me most was the sense of collective humility from the crowd, a warm contentment at the pilgrims' shared journey.

As the kilometres clocked up, I felt a strange sensation of pain in my feet and realised I was in big trouble. The friction caused by my new sandals got worse, and multiple blisters formed on the soles of my feet, a squelching sensation letting me know when each in turn burst. Each step sent sharp jolts of pain through my nerve endings. Feeling a certain self-pity, I quickly copped myself on. Hundreds of thousands were walking barefoot without complaint and many by the roadside seeking alms were devoid of one, two or sometimes even three limbs, placing my pathetic blisters in perspective. Eight kilometres in, I hit my stride and breached the pain barrier. How privileged was I to be there?

We passed countless roadside temples and shrines, each with its own devotees lighting candles and leaving offerings. As the streets narrowed towards the approach to the main entranceway of Arunachaleswarar Temple, the crowd slowed to a snail's pace. There was a bottleneck caused by a barrier ahead, through which only two could fit side by side. I could scarcely believe it as thousands patiently waited their turn to file through. Had this been a similar-sized event in Ireland, tempers would have frayed, and skirmishes broken out, alcohol most likely fuelling heightened tensions. I had policed events with a fraction of people present, and trouble had never been too far away, public order unit vans always parked at the ready.

The next morning, I woke to the sight of Arunachala benignly framed by the window, a swathe of trees circling the visible part of its base. Ditching the sandals, I squeezed my puffy, blistered feet into a comfortable pair of runners, the immediate cushioning effect providing some relief. Breakfast was a glorious fresh fruit salad topped off with traditional yoghurt and pomegranate, a refreshing start to the day.

Returning to Ramana Ashram where the soothing cold stone slabs awaited the stricken soles of my bare feet, once again I was magnetically drawn to the noticeboard on the right of the New Hall, and took up reading from where I left off the day before:

Is the body 'I'? It is silent and inert, but I feel the full force of my personality and even the voice of the 'I' within me, apart from it. So I am spirit transcending the body. The body dies but the spirit that transcends it cannot be touched by death.

That means I am the deathless spirit.' All this was not dull thought: it flashed through me vividly as living truth which I perceived directly, almost without thought process.

I paused there and reread, 'So I am spirit transcending the body.' These few lines, spontaneously divined by a relatively uneducated youth in a remote rural outpost in southeast India, hit on what has captivated scholars, saints, mystics and philosophers for centuries.

'I' was something very real, the only real thing about my present state, and all the conscious activity connected with my body was centred on that 'I'. From that moment onwards, the 'I' or Self focused attention on itself by a powerful fascination. Fear of death had vanished for once and for all.

Absorption in the Self continued unbroken from that time on. Other thoughts might come and go like the various notes of music, but the 'I' continued like the fundamental note that underlies and blends with all the other notes. Whether the body was engaged in talking, reading or anything else, I was still centred on 'I'. Previous to that crisis I had no clear perception of my Self and was not consciously attracted to it. I felt no perceptible or direct interest in it, much less any inclination to dwell permanently in it.

Having read enough for one day, I pulled back, lost in reflection on my own strange engagement with death, from fear, to exposure, to resignation to the notion that it was final and awaited us all eventually. But here in this faraway land of colour, wisdom and humility, another possibility was beginning to take a vague outline in the recesses of my awareness.

The nearby Old Hall was where Ramana Maharshi had stayed for two decades. It was there that devotees had experienced the potent peace that emanated from his presence, the dynamic silence vibrant with his grace. They spoke of the divine love shining from his eyes and how his answers to their questions illuminated them. Concerned that he should be accessible to all, the doors were never closed and even at night people were permitted to come to be with him.

That same hall received visitors from far and wide as news of Ramana Maharshi's saintly wisdom spread. W. Somerset Maugham, for example, visited in 1938 and later used him as the model for the holy man, Shri Ganesha, in his 1944 novel *The Razor's Edge*, subsequently an Oscar-winning movie of the same name starring Tyrone Power and Anne Baxter. Maugham's experiences of meeting Ramana Maharshi were recounted 20 years later in a nonfictional essay titled 'The Saint': 'I have read the autobiography of St Theresa and the lives, written by those who knew them, of St Francis of Assisi, of Catherine of Siena and of Ignatius Loyola. But it never occurred that I might be so fortunate as to meet a saint in the flesh. But that is actually what I did.'

Maugham's account of their encounter is equally inspiring,

After the first few minutes during which his eyes with a gentle benignity rested on my face, he ceased to look at me, but, with a sidelong stare of peculiar fixity, gazed, as it were, over my shoulder. His body was absolutely still, but now and then one of his feet tapped lightly on the earthen floor. He remained thus, motionless, for perhaps a quarter of an hour; and they told me later that he was concentrating in meditation upon me. Then he came to, if I may so put it, and again looked at me. He asked me if I wished to say anything to him or ask any question. I was feeling weak and ill and said so; whereupon he smiled and said, 'Silence is also conversation.'

The Old Hall had probably changed little in the intervening nine decades. It was rectangular in shape, high-ceilinged, a fan in the centre silently keeping the temperature cool, the same large clock marking the ceaseless passage of time, its pendulum still swinging, and the peaceful atmosphere maintained by those who sat here deep in enquiry. The large sofa where Ramana Maharshi had once sat in meditation now supported a life-size oil painting of him in a familiar reclining pose, his compassionate all-knowing eyes surveying the room.

Sitting with my back against the rear wall, I saw that many creeds and religions were represented throughout the hall and marvelled at the atmosphere of respect and silence which prevailed. Closing my own eyes, I reflected on how approximately six weeks after his death experience, the 16-year-old boy had slipped away from home and travelled 320 kilometres (200 miles) by train and foot to reach Arunachala three days later. There he had sheltered in surrounding temples and shrines for two years until, by chance, his uncle heard of a description matching the case of the missing youth. His mother arrived and pleaded for him to return home but to no avail. Soon afterwards, he began to live in various caves on Arunachala, until 1922 when he moved to the foot of the holy hill and what is today Ramana Ashram. As Ramana Maharshi's peaceful brown eyes now held mine, I laughed gently to myself at how this strange journey had me sitting barefoot on a stone slab before a painting of a sage who had left his body in 1950.

The following day at lunch I got talking to a lovely couple named Dev and Sarala. Our conversation turned to health, and I shared my earlier travails with dizziness. They recommended a consultation with the Dwarakamai Siddha Varman Clinic, saying that Siddha, an ancient south Indian medical system, was health- and rejuvenation-oriented and involved a reading of the person rather than the symptoms. I went to make an appointment. While doing so, a lively drum chorus outside caught my attention.

I followed the sound up the incline of a dusty side street where, at an intersection, an attractive woman's face looked down from a large sign affixed to the side of a building. Her dark hair was swept back in the traditional style, and I estimated her age to be mid-fifties at most. It was, I realised, a funeral notice displaying details of her life and funeral arrangements, similar to RIP.ie but in large poster format.

Suddenly the drumming kicked off again – six men in their twenties joyously and furiously alternating between lively and wild in their delivery. Behind them a large canopy stretched out from a residence shading a group of eight from the afternoon sun. The street was blocked off, and lying there in repose, her body shrouded in a beautiful garland of flowers, was the woman from the poster. Her body lay in a see-through glass sarcophagus, a thin silver frame holding the large glass panes in place. Underneath, an air-conditioned unit whirred silently to maintain the necessary temperature inside the structure and preserve the dead wife, mother, sister and friend.

Two six- or seven-year-old lads skidded to a halt on their bikes on the upper side of the dead body freezer box and impassively took in their deceased neighbour in full view on the side of the street, in stark contrast to anything I myself would have experienced as a child. Standing respectfully to one side, I watched as the drummers moved in a fluid formation towards a group of five ladies coming up the street and escorted them towards the funeral party under the canopy. The menfolk looked on stoically while wails of grief and sorrow punctured the silence as the women hugged the family mourners and then in unison sank to the ground in a huddle, their bright clothing merging in the most vivid splashes of greens, purples, reds, oranges and blues. As if on cue, the drummers unleashed a crescendo of percussion and the reverberations of grief were drowned out.

I moved discreetly back down the laneway as the drumming parade signalled to the cortege that the body would soon be departing by hearse for the cemetery over a mile away. At the junction a Toyota Dyna-style pickup slowly emerged, a montage of colourful signage and structure enveloping the flatbed behind the cab, completely unlike the sinister black, silver and chrome vehicles of my childhood. The sides were covered with the most exquisite lengths of swaying flowered garlands extending from canopied roof to truckbed floor. Without a speck of darkness in its presentation, the livery featured vividly painted horses similar to an amusement carnival scene, the subliminal message being that death was not the sinister experience we imagined.

The mourning women had not followed, instead they lined along the junction with the main road. Suddenly, a large firecracker ripped across the roadway in front of them, clouds of colour surging upwards and outwards, a plume of dust and flower petals from the garlands spreading in all directions. They wailed in grief as the funeral wagon left them behind, gyrating drummers leading the way with just the men in accompaniment. Traffic did not cede to the colourful cortege as motorcycles and cars pushed their way past, life continuing in all its vigour as death trundled by. I followed at a respectful distance, the men shredding the garlands from the truck along the roadway. With every step forward, the back flatbed now revealed more of its occupant lying at an angle, head raised, a floral display draped around her neck, the narrow, sharp pleats of her rust-coloured sari slightly visible. Every so often a powerful firecracker explosion detonated, and the plume of marigold petals once again rose from the roadway.

As we neared the burial ground, the cortege swerved obliviously across the central reservation into oncoming traffic and paused. The men, now shorn of their adornments, prepared to remove the remains. As I watched, one suddenly broke away and crossed the road to where I stood.

'Why are you watching?' he asked, his English heavily accented, eyes filled with suspicion.

Quickly estimating his age I asked, 'Was this your mother?'

'Yes,' he replied as he glanced away.

In the universal symbol of respect, I joined my palms. 'I am so sorry for your loss, please pass on my sympathies to your family.'

Looking confusedly at me for what seemed an eternity, there was a flicker of recognition as his sad eyes bore into mine. Suddenly he lunged and threw one arm around my neck, pulling me downward towards him, the other grasping around my back. His head buried against my nape and there we stood, united in a moment of respect.

'Thank you,' he mumbled into the crook of my neck before pulling away just as quickly as he had materialised, retreating across the median to the waiting remains of his mother.

I watched as the cortege disappeared into the cemetery darkness, bobbing phone torches lighting the haphazard route, death like I had never experienced it.

I slept deeply once more that night, but not before reading *The Maharshi and His Message*, Paul Brunton's account of his time at Arunachala with this humble sage who had lived on or by its slopes for all but 16 years of his life. Throughout it, Ramana Maharshi had sought no devotees, demanded no following, issued no commandments. Instead, as Paul Brunton had written, 'The gist of his message is: Pursue the enquiry 'Who Am I?' relentlessly. Analyse your entire personality. Try to find out where the I-thought begins. Go on with your meditations. Keep turning your attention within. One day the wheel of thought will slow down, and an intuition will mysteriously arise. Follow that intuition, let your thinking stop, and it will eventually lead you to the goal.' From direct experience, Ramana Maharshi had affirmed that clarity, peace and contentment was available to all, from deep inside themselves. True understanding was not a prize to be chased after, but our natural state. Like cleaning an old mirror which had appeared to be just a dull piece of glass, self-enquiry removed the layers and allowed us to recognise what we had always been.

In an approach accessible to all, Ramana Maharshi had repeatedly encouraged the simple task of self-investigation, self-enquiry and addressing the core question, 'Who Am I?' I smiled to myself at his constant use of 'investigation' and 'enquiry', words that had formed the basis of my own working life. As my eyes closed and sleep approached, the images and sights of the day flickering across my mind's eye, I mouthed silently, 'To whom do these thoughts belong?'

When I awoke, rested, I focused once more on the framed image of Arunachala outside my window, immovable, timeless, ever-present, in stark contrast to the line of lush foliage at its base swaying and writhing in a stiff warm breeze, symbolic of the restlessness of thoughts, emotions and sensations that consume our daily existence. Later on, I slowly ascended the mountain path to visit Skandashram, the cave where Ramana had lived from 1916 to 1922 overlooking the stunning Arunachaleshwarar Temple below.

Removing my footwear, I entered the crowded cave barefoot, its cool interior a welcome respite from the midday heat. Spying a smaller alcove to the left, I fumbled my way there as my eyes adjusted to the darkness. Sitting with my back to the wall, a concrete plinth to my left, covered with an ochre cloth, bore two large, framed photographs of Ramana Maharshi in his younger years. I relaxed and closed my eyes once more as the vibrant sights and images of the past few days danced across my mind's eye. They were incessant, colourful and fluid, a constant stream of visual imagery unfolding like a cinema reel. I decided to concentrate intently on the simple questions: 'What is this I?' and 'To whom do these thoughts belong?'

I sat for what seemed like ages in the shadows and maybe sleep came to me. Gently squeezing my eyes, to my bewilderment the images started to recede and slowly disappeared. Staying intensely focused as the last one faded, I was left with a picture of utter darkness without even a pinprick of light intruding. Gradually shapes like nothing I had ever seen started to appear – shards of light flowing upwards and outwards from a void the outer reaches of which were like some sort of a large flowing floral beam. Rapt and absorbed by the source of this emanation, I peered into its centre. Was I dreaming? Suddenly the magnitude of the light became spectacular, causing me to catch my breath.

Then I recoiled from the image, and the spell was broken. When I opened my eyes, I found myself alone in the shaded anteroom, Ramana Maharshi's kind eyes looking out from the photos, all seeing, all-knowing. Having never taken hallucinogens to produce altered states of consciousness, the sensation of having experienced something akin to a natural change in my perception of reality stayed with me. My analytical mind kicked in and started to parse what had happened, searching for a logical explanation. It found none. I decided to just let it be. Although not religious, devotional or even spiritual in any shape or form, I have always had the gift to sense, from first contact, the innate character of a person. The converse of this gift is an ability to accurately intuit falsehoods, sharp practices or less-than-genuine intentions. This was invaluable to me during many high-charged encounters throughout my policing life. But never before had it presented in relation to an experience, rather than a person.

All that I could say with total conviction was, that having

earnestly and sincerely carried out the investigation, 'To whom do these thoughts belong?', and followed a variation of the enquiry, 'Who am I?' to its source. It seemed I had actually glimpsed a snippet of what lay beyond the thoughts that consume us each waking hour. I could certainly relate to Ramana Maharshi's observation, 'To ask the mind to kill the mind is like making the thief the policeman. He will go with you and pretend to catch the thief, but nothing will be gained. So you must turn inward and see from where the mind rises and then it will cease to exist ... But instead of setting about saying there is a mind and I want to kill it; you begin to seek the source of the mind and then you find it does not exist at all.'

On the morning of my Siddha consultation, a sign in the spotlessly clean waiting area caught my eye. In large bold print it announced 'No Prior Appointments'. In defiance of the proclamation, however, I was ushered into the office of Dr V. Balasubramanian, who greeted me with a warm and friendly smile. As I outlined the circumstances leading to Dev's recommendation, he silenced me with a wave of his hand. Grabbing my right arm in his and folding my fingers into a fist, he breathed some form of a prayer over my knuckles before beginning to read the patterns of vibration as he unfolded each finger while pulling it to its full length. Then folding each tightly in turn, he located the three different pulse qualities in a single artery on each wrist, before evaluating the strength and vitality of each internal organ through the application of pressure of various levels to the index, middle and ring fingers. Following a quick run of his hands over my arms and legs and a gentle poke in the belly, he called out a series of instructions to his assistant, who noted his diagnosis. He took my blood pressure and only then started to speak directly to me.

'You are very healthy, good heart, great blood pressure, but one small problem.' He paused before demonstrating with his hand in a clutching motion, 'You have a little problem with your capillaries, when you constrict like this with stress.' He prescribed a ginger-based compound to counter the effect. Without having been told about my dizziness issues, he had literally put his finger on the pulse and come up with the same essential conclusion as the consultant neurologist and physiotherapist I had attended back home. A few minutes later my prescription was ready: one teaspoonful twice a day for 30 days would improve me no end, he reassured me. I kept an open mind, willing to consume any potion necessary never to experience that awful dizziness again.

My last day in Tiruvannamalai was reserved for a pilgrimage to Yama Lingam, an impressive temple dedicated to, Yama, the lord of death, which is situated beside the cremation grounds on Chengam road. I thought of his dialogue in the Katha Upanishad with the young boy Nachiketa, whose determination to solve the eternal mystery of death he eventually rewarded with the following words:

The Self is immortal. It was not born, nor does it die. It did not come out of anything, neither did anything come out of it. Even if this body is destroyed, the soul is not destroyed. The one who thinks that he is the slayer and the one who thinks that he is slain, both are ignorant. For the Self neither slays nor is slain. Smaller than the smallest and larger than the largest, the Self is living in all beings.

The knowledge about it can neither be obtained by discussion, nor by brain power, nor even by much learning. It reveals itself to the deserving one. This body is the chariot, intelligence the driver, the senses are the horses, conscience the rein and the soul is the lord of the chariot. The Self is superior to body, mind and senses. Greater than the individual soul is the enveloping super consciousness, the seed of everything in the universe, still greater is the Ultimate Person than whom there is nothing greater. This is the goal of our aspiration.

Once that Supreme Self is realised, death loses all its terrors, and the one who has realised becomes immortal. The path to realisation is long and difficult, like the razor's edge, narrow and sharp. Therefore there is no time to be lost. Awake, arise, bestir yourself and do not stop until the goal is reached.

Yama demonstrated to worshippers that all who were born would someday die, but since they were truly the immortal spirit and not the body, they didn't need to fear death. He was portrayed sitting on his mount, a powerful black buffalo with two monstrous dogs by his side and carried a huge lasso with which he dragged each being at the time of death to face heaven or hell according to their destiny. Standing in front of the doors to the shrine's inner sanctum, I contemplated my own strange trajectory, from childhood fears of death, through a 32-year working life in its closest proximity, before receiving the relatively recent life lesson in the form of perspective, understanding and the fortune of recovered health. I felt truly blessed.

On my way back to Ramana Ashram, distant drumming once

more filled the air. A family in mourning had assembled outside a raised roadside residence. Seeing no glass coffin, I guessed that the deceased was still being prepared inside. The mourners faced the passing traffic and pedestrians in respectful silence, the women in an array of bright colours, the men dressed all in white. An elderly man sat impassively on a raised chair, his grey hair and beard lending a distinguished air to his demeanour. His eyes were closed as if in meditation and a long floral garland brightened his white robes. I suddenly realised that *he* was the deceased, his dark complexion masking the deathly pallor so familiar to me.

Later that night, passing an open area that was occasionally used as a crematorium, I noticed flickering flames inside the pitch-black boundary. I entered the space. Unlike funeral pyres depicted in the movies, this one was low to the ground, just a few feet in height, and the body of the elderly man I had seen in repose only that morning was being consumed by a strong flame underneath, a criss-cross of timber and dried cow dung enclosing him in an oven-type effect. I stood for a moment to pay my respects, wisps of patterned smoke drifting into the darkness as the clay and dust slowly ignited, his final journey of being absorbed back into Arunachala well under way.

The next morning Nagaraj was waiting. I swung my backpack into his taxi, and soon Arunachala was fading into the distance as we headed once more for Chennai International Airport. About halfway there, he asked if I would like to stop for coffee and I replied that I was okay.

'But the coffee is very fine here,' he persisted. So we pulled in for a short break at the next roadside café and soon we were off again, back in the organised chaos of the traffic.

After a few short miles we came across a car lying on its side in the ditch. There were gouges and shards of glass on the asphalt. A crowd had gathered – motorcyclists and other onlookers standing around in shock.

On the hard shoulder lay a woman in green and gold robes and white trousers, the telltale sign of one bare foot, the other shoe still intact, hinting at the level of force involved as she was thrown from the car as it rolled. She was dead, of that I was sure, having witnessed such a scene so many times over the years. While life is still present, people crouch by the person, comforting, reviving, encouraging and helping. When it has passed, they stand shocked, helpless and powerless in the face of death, as they did there on the road to Chennai. Had our short coffee stop saved us from involvement? As the emergency services sped by towards the scene, I closed my eyes and reflected as images rushed by my mind's eye. I tried to focus, to move past the thoughts but I found I couldn't do it; they were too vibrant and strong. So I let them continue their random sequence, content in the awareness that something more profound lay beyond.

As the plane banked, I looked out my window, hoping for a final glimpse of Arunachala in the distance, but the haze over Chennai limited visibility. Reclining, I reflected on the remarkable events that had unfolded following my decision to leave the gardaí and change career, and the invisible doorways that had opened as a result. Most of all, I marvelled at this ultimate investigation, an enquiry into the circumstances surrounding a young boy who had gone missing from his family for two years and whose wisdom had brought me to this faraway land. The sights, images and events of Arunachala danced before me – temples, caves, sages, seekers, pilgrims, beggars, street vendors, funerals, monkeys and holy cows. To whom did these thoughts belong?

# ACKNOWLEDGEMENTS

I would like to extend my deepest gratitude to the following people for their kindness and support. To my wife Jacqui for her patience, understanding, valuable feedback and prescience 20 years ago to repeatedly suggest that I had a book in me. To my son Paul for his early edits (he is a better writer than I will ever be), and my sons Shane and Richard for their interest and encouragement to get started. I am so proud of the amazing adults they have become.

Thank you to my literary agent Faith O'Grady for her wisdom and support and to Seán Hayes for his initial approach after viewing my TEDx talk. Thank you to the team at Gill Books – to Sarah Liddy for her belief in this book and to Margaret Farrelly and Liza Costello for their diligent editing. Thank you to Mary Fleming for her time-pressured work and creative suggestions for the cover.

Thank you to my dear friends Jennifer Burke and Aine Keenan who were a constant source of knowledge, vision and insightful feedback, and who opened my eyes to what I could not see. To my uncle Tommy Murray, a writer, poet and playwright, for his encouragement and background information. To my former colleagues in Crime Scene Investigation – Mark, Ray, Mary, Anne and our late colleague Phil, R.I.P., I thank you for your support and friendship. A special mention for Valerie, whose infectious good humour brightened the aftermath of many a tragic scene. You have all done the State some service.

Thank you to my father, retired Detective Sergeant Pat Prior, a true investigator. To my sister Michelle for her patience, kindness and care for Helena in her final months. To Marian Leonard for her kindness in sharing Esther's diary and allowing it to be reproduced on these pages. To each family of the many departed I have encountered across a lifetime of policing. Please rest assured that your loved ones were considered, thought about and respected during our care, they will never be forgotten.

Ciaran Prior, May 2024.